PCs
FOR
DUMMIES®
QUICK REFERENCE

by Dan Gookin and Sandra Hardin Gookin

Hungry Minds™

Best-Selling Books • Digital Downloads • e-Books • Answer Networks • e-Newsletters •
Branded Web Sites • e-Learning

New York, NY ◆ Cleveland, OH ◆ Indianapolis, IN

PCs For Dummies® Quick Reference

Published by
Hungry Minds, Inc.
909 Third Avenue
New York, NY 10022
www.hungryminds.com
www.dummies.com

Library of Congress Control Number: 00-103392

ISBN: 0-7645-0722-2

Printed in the United States of America

10 9 8 7

1O/SS/QT/QS/IN

Distributed in the United States by Hungry Minds, Inc.

Distributed by CDG Books Canada Inc. for Canada; by Transworld Publishers Limited in the United Kingdom; by IDG Norge Books for Norway; by IDG Sweden Books for Sweden; by IDG Books Australia Publishing Corporation Pty. Ltd. for Australia and New Zealand; by TransQuest Publishers Pte Ltd. for Singapore, Malaysia, Thailand, Indonesia, and Hong Kong; by Gotop Information Inc. for Taiwan; by ICG Muse, Inc. for Japan; by Intersoft for South Africa; by Eyrolles for France; by International Thomson Publishing for Germany, Austria and Switzerland; by Distribuidora Cuspide for Argentina; by LR International for Brazil; by Galileo Libros for Chile; by Ediciones ZETA S.C.R. Ltda. for Peru; by WS Computer Publishing Corporation, Inc., for the Philippines; by Contemporanea de Ediciones for Venezuela; by Express Computer Distributors for the Caribbean and West Indies; by Micronesia Media Distributor, Inc. for Micronesia; by Chips Computadoras S.A. de C.V. for Mexico; by Editorial Norma de Panama S.A. for Panama; by American Bookshops for Finland.

For general information on Hungry Minds' products and services please contact our Customer Care Department within the U.S. at 800-762-2974, outside the U.S. at 317-572-3993 or fax 317-572-4002.

For sales inquiries and reseller information, including discounts, premium and bulk quantity sales, and foreign-language translations, please contact our Customer Care Department at 800-434-3422, fax 317-572-4002, or write to Hungry Minds, Inc., Attn: Customer Care Department, 10475 Crosspoint Boulevard, Indianapolis, IN 46256.

For information on licensing foreign or domestic rights, please contact our Sub-Rights Customer Care Department at 650-653-7098.

For information on using Hungry Minds' products and services in the classroom or for ordering examination copies, please contact our Educational Sales Department at 800-434-2086 or fax 317-572-4005.

Please contact our Public Relations Department at 212-884-5163 for press review copies or 212-884-5000 for author interviews and other publicity information or fax 212-884-5400.

For authorization to photocopy items for corporate, personal, or educational use, please contact Copyright Clearance Center, 222 Rosewood Drive, Danvers, MA 01923, or fax 978-750-4470.

Hungry Minds™ is a trademark of Hungry Minds, Inc.

About the Authors

Dan Gookin considers himself a writer and computer "guru" whose job it is to remind everyone computers are not to be taken too seriously. His approach to computers is light and humorous, yet very informative.

Dan's most recent titles include the best-selling *Word 2000 for Windows For Dummies*, *PCs For Dummies*, 7th Edition, and *Dan Gookin Teaches Windows 98*. He is the author of the original *For Dummies* book, *DOS For Dummies*. All told, he's written over 75 books on computers. Dan currently lives with his wife Sandra (see below) and four sons somewhere in the Pacific Northwest.

Sandra Hardin Gookin has the remarkable ability to make difficult tasks easy to understand. This comes from her Speech Communications degree from Oklahoma State University, but mainly from having to communicate with her 5 boys (4 children + 1 husband, Dan).

Sandra's other books include *Parenting For Dummies*, *How to Use Excel 2000*, *Discover Windows 95*, and *The Illustrated Computer Dictionary For Dummies*.

Together, Dan and Sandra's number one commitment is to their children. However, you can also find them directing and acting in their great community theatre, the Lake City Playhouse.

Authors' Acknowledgments

Many thanks go to the folks at IDG Books who still work to keep us busy. We also want to give our thanks and love to our beautiful boys, Jordan, Simon, Jonah, and Jeremiah. They make us laugh, believe in blessings, and constantly remind us of why we don't allow liquids next to the computer keyboard.

Publisher's Acknowledgments

We're proud of this book; please send us your comments through our Online Registration Form located at www.dummies.com.

Some of the people who helped bring this book to market include the following:

Acquisitions, Editorial, and Media Development

Senior Project Editor: Jodi Jensen

Acquisitions Editor: Ed Adams

Copy Editors: Gwenette Gaddis, Nicole Laux

Proof Editor: Teresa Artman

Technical Editor: Lee Musick

Editorial Manager: Kyle Looper

Editorial Assistant: Sarah Shupert

Production

Project Coordinator: Nancee Reeves

Layout and Graphics: Amy Adrian, Jill Piscitelli, Brian Torwelle

Proofreaders: Corey Bowen, Vickie Broyles, Charles Spencer York Production Services, Inc.

Indexer: York Production Services, Inc.

Special Help
Sheri Replin, Jeremy Zucker

General and Administrative

Hungry Minds Technology Publishing Group: Richard Swadley, Vice President and Executive Group Publisher; Bob Ipsen, Vice President and Group Publisher; Joseph Wikert, Vice President and Publisher; Barry Pruett, Vice President and Publisher; Mary Bednarek, Editorial Director; Mary C. Corder, Editorial Director; Andy Cummings, Editorial Director

Hungry Minds Manufacturing: Ivor Parker, Vice President, Manufacturing

Hungry Minds Marketing: John Helmus, Assistant Vice President, Director of Marketing

Hungry Minds Production for Branded Press: Debbie Stailey, Production Director

Hungry Minds Sales: Michael Violano, Vice President, International Sales and Sub Rights

Contents at a Glance

Table of Contents

The Personal Computer

The Big Picture. Of what? The Big Picture of a PC. Your personal computer. Consider this your personal tour of what your computer looks like, what you'll see as you snoop around the front and back of the console, and what you can do with that big boxy thing sitting on your desk.

In this part, you enter a personal computer basic training course. Remember, only the tough survive, so keep reading.

In this part . . .

✓ What You See

✓ The Basics

✓ What You Can Do

What You See: Basic Hardware

First of all, you need a computer. If you already own one and are ready to get started, you've come to the right place. The following figure shows you what a typical computer system looks like. I've flagged the basic pieces, and I tell you more about them in the list that follows.

- **Console:** This main computer box is also known as the *system unit*. It contains your computer's guts, plus various buttons, lights, and holes into which you plug the rest of the computer system.

- **Monitor:** This is the TV-set-like thing on which the computer displays information.

- **Mouse:** This is the device that lets you work with graphical objects that the computer displays on the monitor's screen. *See also* Part II to find out more about working with the mouse.

- **Keyboard:** It's the thing you type on. *See also* Part II for more information about the keyboard.

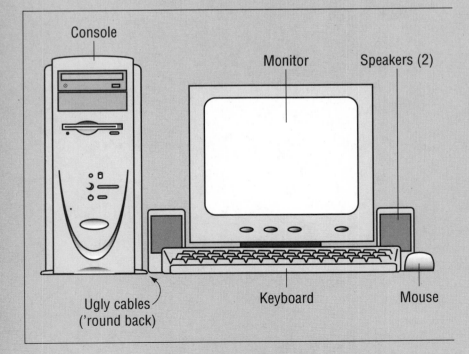

- ✔ **Speakers:** Most PCs can bleep and squawk through a set of stereo speakers, either external ones that you set up or ones built into the console or monitor.

- ✔ **Printer:** It's where you get the computer's output — the printed stuff, also called *hard copy*. **See also** Part VII to find out more about printing your work.

- ✔ **Lots of ugly cables:** These are what computer salespeople never show you — the ganglia of cables that live behind your computer. These cables are required so that you can plug things into the wall and into each other.

You may have also heard of something called a CPU, which is one of those cute acronyms for *central processing unit*. The CPU is really the computer's main chip.

If you don't own a PC but are in the market for one, check out *Buying a Computer For Dummies,* written by yours truly and published by IDG Books Worldwide, Inc. This book covers the basics of the PC, how to select one that's just right for you, and how to set it up for the first time.

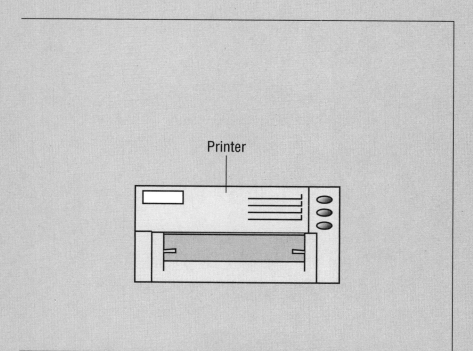

Printer

What You See: Console — the Front

The console is the most important part of your computer. It's the Big Box. Every part of your computer system either lives inside the console or plugs into it. The following figure shows what a typical PC console looks like. I've flagged the more interesting places to visit, although you may find them in a different location on your computer than what you see in the figure.

- **CD-ROM or DVD drive:** This drive accepts data and music CDs in addition to DVDs. The high-capacity discs used in the CD-ROM or DVD drives look exactly like music CDs, but they contain computer information.

- **Future expansion:** You can add lots of different things to your computer, and most consoles have plenty of room to accommodate these future additions. Blank areas or cover plates on the front of your computer mean that you can add drives and other things (such as a tape backup) later.

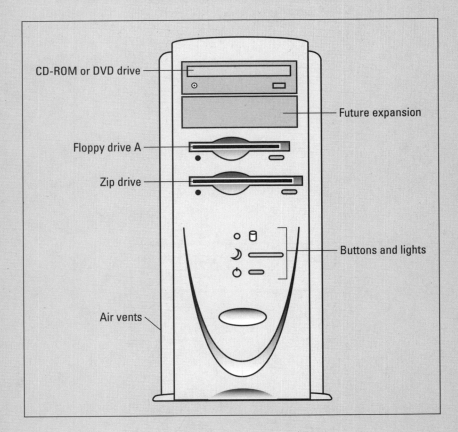

- **Floppy drive:** This slot eats floppy disks. Some software comes on floppy disks, and you can also use these disks to move files from one PC to another.

- **Zip drive:** A common option found on many PCs, the Zip drive is like a super-duper floppy drive. You can store the equivalent of 100 floppy disks worth of information on a Zip disk.

- **Air vents:** Most consoles sport some type of air vent on the front. Don't block the air vents with books or sticky notes! Let it breathe.

- **Buttons and lights:** Most of the computer's buttons are on the keyboard. A few of the more important ones, however, are on the console. On fancier PCs, these buttons are accompanied by many impressive tiny lights. These buttons and lights include the following:

- **On-off button:** This is the PC's main power button: the one you use to turn the darn thing on.

- **Reset button:** This button lets you restart the computer without going through the bother of turning it off and then on again.

- **Sleep button:** This is a feature on some newer PCs and most laptops. Pressing this button causes your PC to go into a coma, suspending all activity without turning the computer off.

- **Hard drive light:** This light flashes when the hard drive is working.

Other unusual things may live on the front of your console, such as other types of removable drives, locks and keys, turbo buttons, and stickers that say "I was built to run Windows 98" or "A Pentium lurks inside this box." Unfortunately, you seldom find a Panic button.

The on-off symbol may indicate the Reset button on some computers. So much for international symbols! Check with your computer manual to be sure.

What You See: Console — the Back

The back of the console is where you find a variety of connectors for the many other devices in your computer system: a place to plug in the monitor, keyboard, mouse, speakers, and just about anything else that came in the box with the PC.

Power connector: The power cord that plugs into the wall gets connected here.

 Keyboard connector: The keyboard plugs into this little hole.

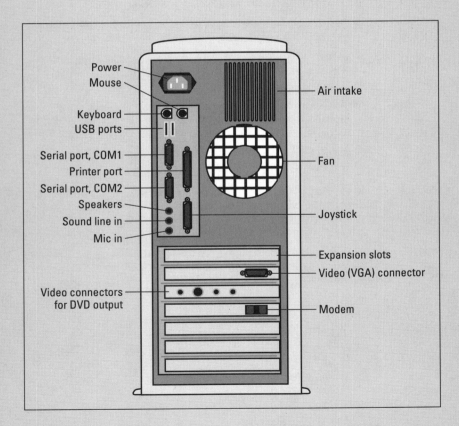

Power
Mouse
Keyboard
USB ports
Serial port, COM1
Printer port
Serial port, COM2
Speakers
Sound line in
Mic in
Video connectors for DVD output

Air intake
Fan
Joystick
Expansion slots
Video (VGA) connector
Modem

Mouse connector: This hole is generally the same size and shape as the keyboard connector, but it has a mouse icon nearby to tell you that the mouse plugs in here.

 USB port: Plug your USB devices into these tiny slots.

 Serial (or COM) ports: Most PCs have two of these ports, labeled COM1 and COM2. This is where you plug in an external modem or sometimes a mouse. A serial port has nine holes.

 Printer port: You plug your printer into this connector.

Joystick port: This port may be identified by an image, or it may say *Joystick* or *Game controller*.

Monitor connector: Your PC's monitor plugs into this hole. Sometimes, the hole is on an expansion slot and is unlabeled. If so, you can tell which is the monitor connector because it has 15 little holes in it — more than the serial port.

Speaker/sound-out jack: This is where you plug in your PC's external speakers; you can also use this jack to hook up the PC to a sound system.

Line-in jack: This is where you plug your stereo or VCR into the PC to capture sound.

Microphone jack: You plug the computer's microphone into this hole.

Modem: Two connectors live on the modem. One is for connecting the modem to the phone jack in your wall; the other is to connect a telephone so that you can answer the phone.

S-Video out: If your PC sports a DVD drive, it may have several additional connectors for video output. The S-Video connector lets you connect a TV to your PC (if the TV has an S-Video connector). Other video connectors let you pump a DVD movie out to a TV or VCR.

In addition to the ports and jacks, the back of the console includes expansion slots. These slots are the backsides of various expansion cards that you can plug into your PC. Some expansion slots have connectors (like the video connectors shown in the figure) that let you plug in other goodies.

After you've located all these holes and plugs, you can start plugging things in. There is no *proper* order to this process. Just make sure that your computer is OFF. Now when you flip the power switch, everything is ready to go.

The Basics: What Is a PC?

Technically, a PC is a large calculator. Of course, the display is better and it has a ton more buttons. PCs are also as proficient at working with words as they are with numbers. And even though laptop and notebook computers are lighter and more portable, they are still considered PCs.

You can use a computer for a number of different tasks; in the process, you can solve an infinite number of problems in a number of creative ways. Just about anything that you can do with words, numbers, information, or communication, you can do with a computer.

In a way, a computer is just another electronic gadget. But unlike your toaster, a personal computer can be *programmed* to do a number of interesting tasks. It's up to you to tell the computer what you want it to do, making a computer's potential limitless. Remember these important things about PCs:

- You never have to learn about programming to use a computer. Someone else does the programming; then you buy the program (the software) to get your work done.

- Your job, as the computer operator, is to tell the software what to do, which then tells the computer what to do.

Hardware

Two separate things make up a computer: hardware and software. They go hand in hand. You cannot have one without the other.

Hardware is the physical part of a computer, anything you can touch and anything you can see. Yet, hardware is nothing unless it has software to control it. In a way, hardware is like a car without a driver or a saw without a carpenter; you need both to make something happen.

 If you can throw it out a window, it's hardware. For example, disks themselves are hardware; software is what is recorded on the disk. Similarly, a CD isn't music; the music is what's recorded on the CD. The CD is hardware.

Software

Software is the brains of the computer. It tells the hardware what to do. Without software, hardware just sits around bored and unappreciated. You must have software to make a computer go. In fact, software determines your computer's personality. Remember these important points about software:

- Computer software is nothing more than instructions that tell the hardware what to do, how to act, or when to lose your data. Without the proper software, your computer is merely an expensive doorstop.

✔ Although computer software comes on disks (CDs or floppy disks), the *disks* aren't the software. Software is stored on disks just as music is stored on cassettes and CDs.

The operating system

The *operating system* is the most important piece of software. The operating system rules the computer, controlling all the individual computer components and making sure that everything gets along well. It's the actual brains of the operation, telling the nitwitted hardware what to do next.

The operating system also controls *applications* software. Each of those programs must bend a knee and take a loyalty oath to the operating system.

The operating system typically comes with the computer when you buy it. You never need to add a second operating system, although operating systems do get updated and improved from time to time. It's pretty likely that your PC includes some version of Microsoft Windows as its operating system, such as Windows 95, Windows 98, Windows NT, Windows 2000 Professional, or Windows Millennium.

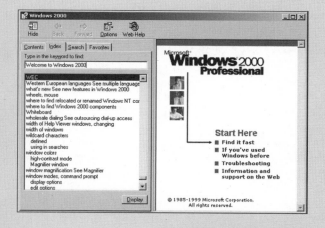

When you buy software, you buy it for an operating system, not for your brand of PC. So most users buy software that runs on either a Macintosh or Windows system. A system called *Linux* also exists, but software isn't as readily available for this newer operating system.

The Basics: Turning On the Computer

To turn on the computer, follow this simple step:

Push the On button.

That's it. Finding the computer switch is really the toughest part of turning the computer on. Most PCs put the switch on the front of the console, but on others, you may find the switch on the side or even on the back.

Some switches are the on-off flip or "rocker" type. Other switches are a push button that you use to turn the system both on and off. You may find the newer computers are equipped with a main power switch on the back of the console and the on/off button on the front.

 If the computer doesn't turn on, check to see whether it's plugged in.

The Basics: Turning On More Things

Most of the things connected to your PC have an on-off switch. You should turn these basic components on in this order:

1. Turn on the *monitor* first so that it can warm up.

2. Turn on any *peripherals* — external devices that you plan to use, such as a printer, scanner, external disk drives, and digital camera — so that the computer will "see" them after it's up and running.

3. Turn on the *console* last.

Or you can turn everything on at once by flipping a single switch on a power strip, which is also okay. Generally speaking, however, the console should come on last.

The Basics: Turning Off the Computer

Windows insists that you shut down properly, or it comes back with a message telling you that you didn't do it right. Simply flipping the power switch to the Off position isn't a good idea because you may lose unsaved information. If you don't shut down properly, you may eventually mess up your computer.

Follow these steps to shut down Windows the right way:

1. Click the Start button. The Start button is in the bottom-left corner of the taskbar.

   The best and most reliable way to make the Start menu appear is to press the Ctrl+Esc key combination. It works every time, and it's especially useful when the Start button isn't visible on your screen (if your taskbar is hidden, for example). Or your new keyboard may sport the Windows key which, when pressed, also brings up the Start menu. The Windows key is placed between the Ctrl and Alt key and has that memorable Windows logo on it.

2. Click Shut Down. The Shut Down Windows dialog box appears, offering you additional options for shutting down your PC.

3. Ensure that the Shut Down option is selected as it is in the figure. The item is selected properly when the circle next to the option has a black dot in the center. If it's not selected on your screen, click the mouse pointer anywhere on the Shut Down option to place the dot within the circle, which selects the option.

4. Click the OK button. Windows is outta here! Bye-bye. If you haven't saved the information in any open programs, Windows tells you about it. Go ahead and save everything. Eventually, after more disk commotion than seems necessary, you see a screen that tells you, and I quote, It's now safe to turn off your computer. (*See also* Part VI to find out more about saving files.)

5. Flip the big red switch. Click. You're done. (By the way, the switch on your computer may not be red, but "big red switch" sounds better than "big whatever-colored switch you have on your computer." Ya know?)

Newer PCs may actually go into Sleep mode or shut themselves off automatically. If that's the case, you may not see the It's now safe to turn off your computer message, and you don't have to do Step 5 of the preceding list. You may still have to switch off your monitor, printer, and other devices around the PC.

Never turn off a computer when you're in the middle of something! Always exit your programs, and then shut down Windows properly. The only time you can safely turn off your PC is when the screen tells you that it's safe to do so. *See also* Part III to find out how to exit a program.

Resetting your computer

You may need to reset your computer if it starts acting strange, or freezes up, and nothing seems to work. Resetting is like a good, swift kick to the hiney to get things going again. It's actually a quick way to stop and then restart your computer.

Follow these steps to reset your computer:

1. Click the Start button.

2. Choose Shut Down.

3. Click the dot next to Restart.

You can also use these options for resetting your computer:

✔ Press the Ctrl+Alt+Delete keys at the same time (that means the Control key plus the Alt key plus the Delete key). I don't recommend this method, and you should do this only if your mouse has frozen and you can't get to the Start button.

✔ Push the Reset switch located on your computer console. Not every computer has one of these, and pressing it may just shut down your computer. I don't recommend this method either.

Never reset your computer to get out of an application (unless your program is frozen and you can't get out of it any other way). Never reset while you're in the middle of a program. And never reset when the disk drive light is on. And don't forget to remove any floppy disks from your floppy drive before you reset. And don't forget to floss after brushing your teeth.

Putting your monitor to sleep

Putting your monitor to sleep shuts it off and saves power after a period of inactivity. The PC simply stops sending a signal to the monitor and the monitor goes blank — as if it weren't working.

Follow these steps to put your monitor to sleep:

1. Click the Start button.

2. Choose Settings.

3. Click Control Panel.

4. Double-click the Power Management icon. The Power Management Properties dialog box opens.

5. Choose a time to shut down the monitor. You choose the time near the bottom of the dialog box next to Turn Off Monitor. Click the drop-down arrow for more time options.

6. Click OK to close the dialog box.

7. Close the Control Panel by clicking the X in the upper-right corner.

Now your monitor will sleep after a given period of inactivity. So when you're away from the computer for a while, the monitor will stop displaying an image. This doesn't turn the monitor off; it merely stops displaying an image. You still need to push the monitor's Off button to turn it off.

Suspending your PC

Suspending your computer is putting your whole computer to sleep without turning it off. This is an energy-saving mode that supplies just enough power to keep memory going so that your computer remembers what you just did. But it doesn't keep all the lights and sounds alive, thus saving power.

Follow these steps to suspend your computer:

1. Click the Start button.

2. (For Windows 95) Click the Suspend option.

   (For Windows 98) Choose Shut Down; then choose the Stand By option.

   (For Windows 2000) Choose Shut Down; then choose the Stand By option.

3. Click OK. Your PC looks like it was just switched off, but it's not really off. It's just suspended.

When you're tired of watching your computer do nothing, press any key on the keyboard (the Enter and spacebar keys are my favorites) or jiggle the mouse. Either one of these actions will revive your computer.

 If, for some bizarre reason, your computer enters this suspend mode and won't come out of it (which has been known to happen), you have to reset your computer.

The Basics: Application Programs

By itself, an operating system doesn't really do anything for you. To get work done, you need an *application program*. Application programs do the work. Whatever it is you do on your computer, you do it using an application program. These programs include word processors, spreadsheets, and databases. Other types of programs include utilities, games, and educational and programming software. And then you have all the Internet applications: Web browsers, e-mail programs, and software of that ilk.

The Basics: Types and Models of PCs

Not all computers look like the image shown at the beginning of this Big Picture section. The type of PC shown there is currently the most popular, called the *mini-tower*. The console can sit upright on your desk or be tucked away out of sight beneath the desk; it's sleek and sexy.

PCs are not all configured as mini-towers. For the first ten years or so after the PC came into existence, the desktop model was the most popular. But there are plenty of other models to choose from, each with an orientation, size, and enough blinking lights to please just about anyone.

The following list describes the various types and models of PCs:

- **Mini-tower:** This is currently the most popular PC configuration. The console sits upright on a desktop or beneath the desk.

- **Desktop:** Formerly the most popular PC configuration, this model has a slab-like console that lies flat on the tabletop with the monitor squatting on top.

- **Desktop (small footprint):** A smaller version of the desktop, this is typically used in low-priced home systems. (A PC's *footprint* is the amount of desk space it uses.) A small footprint desktop model is just smaller than the full-size desktop model. In the end, it makes no difference: The amount of clutter you have always expands to fill the available desk space.

- **Notebook or laptop:** This is a specialty type of computer that folds into a handy, lightweight package, ideal for lugging around airports. Laptop PCs work just like their desktop brethren.

- **Towers:** This is essentially a full-sized desktop model standing on its side, making it tall, like a tower. Manufacturers are phasing out this model and going straight to the mini-tower (which is about ten inches shorter than the tower model).

The Basics: The Windows Desktop

Windows is basically full of pictures (otherwise known as *graphics* or *icons*) that you click when you want to select something. All these pictures (or graphics) are on what is called the *desktop*. What you see on the desktop are icons that represent programs in your computer. Double-click one of these icons, and you start that program. You can change the way your desktop looks, and you can decide (somewhat) what goes on your desktop. Ah, the power. *See also* Part XIV to find out some of the fun stuff you can do with your computer.

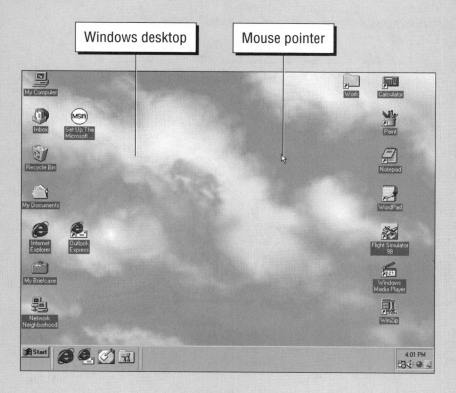

Windows desktop

Mouse pointer

The Basics: The Explorer Window

Windows Explorer (often referred to simply as *Explorer*) is a great way to view, organize, and manipulate your files and folders. It's the best birds-eye view of everything you've stored in your computer. From Explorer, you can cut, copy, paste, or move any file or folder from one place to another.

The following figure shows the open Explorer window. The disk drives and folders in your computer are shown on the left side of the window, and the files and embedded folders are displayed on the right.

Follow these steps to find Windows Explorer:

1. Click the Start button.

2. Choose Programs.

3. Choose Windows Explorer.

Explorer is a prime example of a *tree structure* of files and folders. The root of the structure is the hard drive. From the root come branches of folders, and from those folders, more folders and branches of files.

The Basics: The Start Button

The Start button is the door to all the programs and games that lurk in your computer. Click once on the Start button (located at the bottom-left of your screen), and you open a *menu*. Hover your mouse over one of the words on the menu that has an arrow next to it, and a *submenu* appears. Keep hovering your mouse over more words with more arrows, and more submenus appear. If you ever find anything that excites you (such as a particular program name), simply click it and that program starts for you.

The Basics: The Taskbar

The taskbar is that gray strip at the bottom of your screen that acts as a calling card to the programs that are currently running. Open a program, and you see an icon and a button on the taskbar. Close the program, and the icon and button go away. Want to switch to another program? Just click the icon on the taskbar. (Of course, you have already opened the program to put the button there to begin with, but you knew that.)

Also nestled on the taskbar are the Start button, the Quick Launch bar, and the system tray. Check out the following figure to see all these goodies and to help you spot your taskbar, too. *See also* Part III, "Getting Started with Windows."

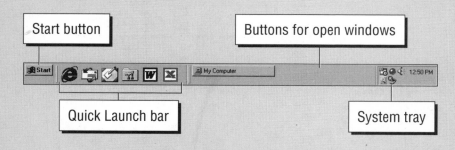

Start button

Buttons for open windows

Quick Launch bar

System tray

What You Can Do: Add a Shortcut Icon to Your Desktop

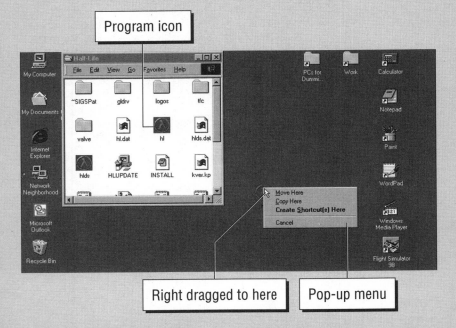

Program icon

Right dragged to here

Pop-up menu

A computer is a tool to help you get work done. To make your work easier, you can place on the desktop shortcuts to programs you use most frequently. To place a program shortcut on your Windows desktop, you can

1. Get started by

Finding Explorer, Part V

Finding your program, Part V

Selecting the program, Part VI

2. Work on your project by

Practicing using the mouse, Part II

Practicing dragging files, Part II

3. Add finishing touches by

Changing the program shortcut, Part III

18

What You Can Do: Use the Internet to Schedule a Flight

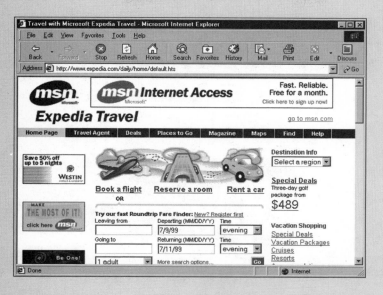

The Internet has changed the way we shop, work, and play. We now have the ability to do fun things, like schedule a vacation, all from the comfort of our homes. To use the Internet to schedule a flight, you can

1. Get started by

Choosing an Internet browser, Part IX

Connecting to the Internet, Part IX

2. Work on your project by

Deciding where you want to go (sorry, I can't help you much with this one)

Finding out details about the location by surfing the Web, Part IX

E-mailing a friend to go with you, Part IX

3. Add finishing touches by

Scheduling your flight, Part IX

What You Can Do: Send a Picture through E-Mail

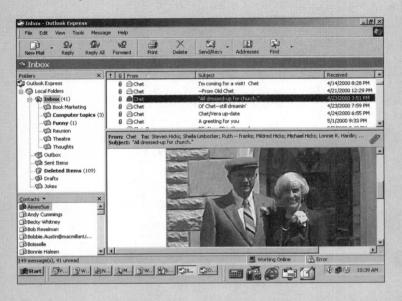

E-mail has been a breakthrough in communication among family and friends. People are staying in touch better because they don't have to go through that envelope and stamp-licking process. And it's also getting easier to send pictures of yourself through e-mail. You just need to be equipped with the proper gadgets, some fun pictures, and e-mail (of course), and you're on your way. To send a picture through e-mail, you can

1. Get started by

Opening the Paint program from the Accessories folder, Part III

Creating a folder for pictures, Part V

Creating a picture and saving it, Part VI

2. Work on your project by

Starting an e-mail message, Part IX

Attaching your picture, Part IX

3. Add finishing touches by

Installing a scanner so that you can access more pictures, Part XI

Plugging Stuff In

The back of your computer has a host of holes and plug-in places. That side of your PC probably faces the wall because it's a ghastly sight. Yet this ugly sight of holes and plugs help you expand your PC system, as well as connect various important items to the main console unit. Officially, these holes are known as *jacks*, or *ports* (which are just other terms for *hole*).

In this part . . .

A Jack Is a Jack Is a Jack

Located on the back of your PC is a hole, lovingly called a *jack*, which is the same thing as a connector. You can plug into the jack any one of a variety of external devices with which your computer can communicate.

Some jacks, known as *ports*, can connect to a variety of things. Others are dedicated to particular devices.

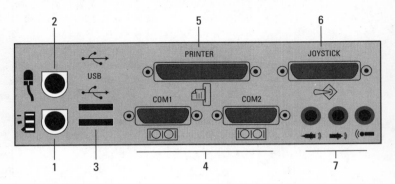

This figure illustrates a panel you would see on the backs of many PCs. This is where you find all the common jacks. More jacks can be found on various expansion cards, but most can be found in one place. You should find these things (the numbers in the following list correspond to the numbers in the figure):

1. Keyboard connector

2. Mouse connector

3. USB port connector (usually two of them)

4. Serial port connector (usually two of them)

5. Printer (parallel) port connector

6. Joystick port connector

7. Audio connectors (three of them)

More ports can be added to any PC through an expansion card. For example, for the price of an expansion card (the going rate is around $60 to $70), you can add a USB port to your computer.

Audio Connectors

Most PCs are sold with audio jacks. These audio jacks enable you to connect all the fun stuff, such as a microphone or external speakers.

 You connect the PC's speakers at the line-out or speaker jack. Some speakers are hooked up to the PC's monitor.

You plug in a microphone into the microphone jack. This enables you to record your voice.

Any other external sound-producing device you may want to connect to your PC is done through the line-in jack.

The Keyboard and the Mouse

The keyboard and mouse jacks look identical on most PCs, so look for the little keyboard and mouse pictures above or below the jacks to guide you in plugging in these devices.

If you have a serial mouse, you have to plug it into the computer's serial port. Plug it into COM1; COM2 is often used as the modem port, and plugging the mouse into COM2 can cause problems. If your PC has a COM3 port, you may plug your serial mouse into it instead of COM1.

If your PC uses a USB mouse, plug it into the USB port. Many PCs have a spare USB port on the keyboard.

 Turn your computer off before you connect or disconnect the mouse.

The Printer Port

You plug your printer into (surprise, surprise) the printer port. Generally, the port displays a little picture of a printer so that you know that you have the right port. The printer cable has two ends: one that plugs into the printer and one that plugs into the computer. If you look carefully, you'll notice that the connectors are different, making it somewhat impossible to plug a printer cable in backwards.

 You won't see this on your printer box, but you have to buy the printer cables that your printer requires. This is a separate purchase. You won't find them hidden in your printer box anywhere. Sorry, you'd think they'd take care of that!

The printer port can also be used as a link to certain external devices, such as CD-ROMs, DVDs, or external tape drives.

The Scuzziest Port of All: SCSI

The SCSI (Small Computer System Interface) port is the fastest port available on many PCs. (Some would argue that a SCSI port doesn't come close to the speed and flexibility of the newer USB port, but that's a topic for a later section.) The SCSI port gives you the capability to connect multiple devices by using a *daisy chain* configuration in which devices are chained to one another, with the final device being connected to the SCSI port. This connection method enables one circuit board or card to handle all the devices instead of requiring a separate card for each device. SCSI technology is continually evolving, so the number of devices that you connect to a single port depends on the type of SCSI port available in your computer. The initial SCSI port, for example, SCSI-1, supported 8 peripherals; the newest standard, Ultra160/m, supports up to 16 devices.

Here are the kinds of devices that you can connect to a SCSI port:

- CD-ROM, CD-R (recordable CD-ROM), and CD-RW (rewritable CD-ROM) drives
- Hard drive
- Removable hard drive or magneto-optical disk drive
- Scanner
- Tape backup drive

SCSI ports are great for PC users who don't mind tinkering with their equipment. The SCSI port can be a challenge to configure because each SCSI device must have its own ID number, and you have to attach a gadget called a *terminator* to the device at the end of the daisy chain.

The following table shows the various types of SCSI ports and their characteristics:

SCSI Type	Max. Cable Length (Meters)	Max. Number of Connections	Speed (Megabytes per Second)
SCSI-1	6	8	5
SCSI 2	6	8 or 16	5–10
Fast SCSI-2	3	8	10–20
Wide SCSI-2	3	16	10–20
Fast Wide SCSI-2	3	16	10–20
Ultra SCSI-3 8-bit	1.5	8	20

SCSI Type	Max. Cable Length (Meters)	Max. Number of Connections	Speed (Megabytes per Second)
Ultra SCSI-3 16-bit	1.5	16	40
Ultra-2 SCSI	12	8	40
Wide Ultra-2 SCSI	12	16	80
Ultra-3 SCSI	12	16	160

Serial (or COM) Ports

Serial ports are an extremely versatile type of connector on your PC. (Some people argue that the USB port is the most versatile, but you can decide that for yourself if you read the next section.) The serial port can have a ton of cool things plugged into it, which is why it has earned the reputation of being so versatile.

You can typically plug the following things into a serial port:

✔ Mouse

✔ Modem

✔ Serial printer

✔ Scanner

✔ Digital camera

You can plug just about anything that requires two-way communication into a serial port. An external modem, however, is the most common device plugged into this port. Because of this fact, serial ports are also called COM ports, which stands for *communication*.

Computers can have up to four serial ports but typically come with two: COM1 and COM2.

USB — The Versatile Port

The most versatile port on your PC is the USB port. Unlike most other ports, USB (Universal Serial Bus) was designed to host a number of different and interesting devices, making it possible to replace just about every other connector on the back of the PC. Microsoft incorporated USB drivers in its Windows 98 operating system, and most new computers and peripheral devices include USB technology. One of the biggest advantages of the USB port is that it requires no configuration. In true *plug-and-play* fashion, you simply plug in a USB device and begin using it. You don't even have to turn off your computer before plugging in the device; your computer recognizes it without rebooting. One additional bonus: unlike your printer and some other peripherals, USB devices all come with their own cables. Yee-ha!

Using the USB

Before you can use a USB device, you have to make sure that your PC has one or more USB connectors. Check the back of your PC for a small, oval port that displays the USB symbol.

Next, you need a USB device. These are external devices that plug into the USB port, such as a monitor, scanner, digital camera, floppy drive, speakers, or whatever you choose to add. Look on the packaging to make sure that your new gadget is a USB device (it will say so — somewhere).

Connecting the USB

As I mentioned earlier, Windows automatically recognizes and configures a USB device when you plug it into a USB port — all without you even turning off or resetting your PC. This should impress you because not all connectors on your PC can do this.

Some older computers that shipped with Windows 95 may have a USB port, but it may not be active. You may have to either upgrade to Windows 98 or install the right drivers for Windows 95 to activate this port.

You don't have to preinstall any new USB device. You can simply plug them in as you need them. So if you already have a USB digital camera plugged in, for example, and now you want to use your USB scanner, simply unplug the camera and plug in the scanner. Presto! You're ready to go. You won't get any nasty warning messages, and your computer won't (well, at least shouldn't) freeze up when you do this.

Some USB devices, such as scanners, plug right into the computer and don't require their own power cord. Instead, these devices use power from the console. This isn't true for all USB devices. USB monitors, for example, usually require a separate power cable.

The USB interface is not the solution for all peripherals. The USB port's speed is still too slow to work with fast hard disk drives. This problem may be solved in the future, however.

Expanding the USB

Most PCs have two USB connectors, so you can plug in two
USB devices. If you have more USB devices, you can unplug and
replug devices as necessary. If you want to connect more than
two USB devices to your PC simultaneously, you have a couple
of options:

 ✔ Buy a USB expansion card and add more USB ports to your PC.

 ✔ Buy a USB hub, which is a device that plugs into your PC's USB
   port and provides multiple jacks for additional USB peripherals.
   With a USB hub, you can add up to 127 peripherals to your PC.

Part II

Working with the Keyboard and Mouse

The computer looks nice, but unless you have a keyboard and mouse, your computer isn't going to do much other than just sit.

The keyboard and mouse are the tools you use to make things happen in programs. You type something by using the keyboard, and click something by using the mouse. Your computer is useless without them.

In this part . . .

Keyboard

The typical PC keyboard is shown in the following figure, although what is considered "typical" is quickly changing. What you see here is called the Enhanced 104-key keyboard. Although the shape of this 104-key keyboard has been changing to provide better support to wrists, keyboards basically still have 104 keys.

Function keys

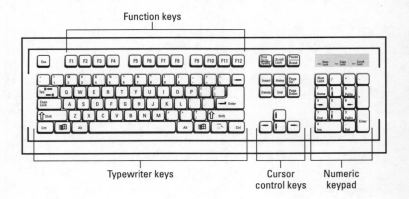

Typewriter keys   Cursor   Numeric
                      control keys   keypad

Keyboard layout

Keyboards include the following four main areas:

✔ **Function keys:** These keys are located on the top row of the keyboard and are labeled from F1 through F12.

✔ **Typewriter keys:** With a few exceptions, such as Alt, Ctrl, and (on some keyboards) a couple of special Windows keys, these are the same keys that you find on a typewriter: letters, numbers, and punctuation symbols. *See also* "The Windows key" and "The Shortcut Menu key" sections later in this part.

✔ **Cursor-control keys:** These four keys are commonly referred to as *arrow keys*. You can use them to move the cursor in the direction in which the arrow is pointing: up, down, left, or right. Above the arrow keys are the Insert, Delete, Home, End, PgUp (page up), and PgDn (page down) keys. *See also* "Editing keys" later in this part to find out what each key does.

✔ **Numeric keypad:** The numeric keypad contains additional number keys laid out as they appear on a calculator keypad. The following math symbols are available on the numeric keypad:

- + is for addition

- – is for subtraction

- * is for multiplication

- / is for division

You can also use the numeric keypad to act as a cursor control device. Press the Num Lock key (on many keyboards, a light appears above or near the Num Lock key, indicating that Num Lock is turned on and the numeric keypad is engaged) to make the numbers work. Press the Num Lock key again to turn off the numeric keypad so that you can use the arrow keys (as labeled) to move the cursor around. The Num Lock key is a *toggle* key — pressing it once turns Num Lock on; pressing it again turns Num Lock off.

The Any key

The screen says, `Press any key to continue.` Hmmm. Any key? Where is the Any key?

Any key refers to, literally, any key on your keyboard. To be safe, however, press the spacebar or the Enter key when your screen says to press "any key."

The Windows key

If you're using Windows 95 or later, it's likely that your keyboard has a few additional keys, such as the Windows key. The Windows key sits between the Alt and Ctrl keys on either side of the spacebar and serves the same purpose as pressing Ctrl+Esc — it pops up the Start menu. When pressed with other keys, the Windows key provides a shortcut to various functions. The following table shows what these key combinations do.

Key Combo	Function
Win+D	Displays the desktop (this may not work for Windows 95)
Win+E	Starts Windows Explorer
Win+F	Displays the Find Files dialog box
Win+R	Displays the Run dialog box

The Shortcut Menu key

The Shortcut Menu key, located between the Windows key and the Ctrl key on the right side of your keyboard, displays the shortcut menu for whatever item is currently selected on the screen. This key works the same as if you had right-clicked an item.

The Enter key

Your PC sports not one, but two, Enter keys. The first one is located just to the right of the quotation mark/apostrophe key. The second Enter key is placed to the right of the numeric keypad for speedy entry of numbers.

You use the Enter key for these things:

✔ To select the highlighted option in a dialog box

✔ To end a paragraph in a word processing program

✔ When you're instructed to "press any key"

Don't press Enter after filling in a text box inside a dialog box. In some cases, pressing Enter closes the dialog box. Use the Tab key to move from text box to text box.

The Tab key

The Tab key is used in two different ways:

✔ To indent paragraphs in a word processing program.

✔ To move between fields or areas in a dialog box. Press Tab instead of Enter, for example, to hop between the First and Last Name fields. This also holds true for filling in a form on the Internet: press Tab, not Enter, to fill in the blanks.

Tabs are considered single, separate characters. When you back-space over a tab in a word processing program, the tab disappears in one chunk — not space by space.

The Escape key

The Windows Escape key (shown as Esc on your keyboard) acts the same as clicking Cancel when you're in a dialog box. It also closes most windows.

Editing keys

When you type text in a Windows document, you can change it, and Windows provides special editing keys to make changing text fast and easy.

The following table lists the common keys and key combinations that you can use for editing text.

Key/Key Combo	Function
←	Moves the text cursor left (back) one character.
→	Moves the text cursor right (forward) one character.
↑	Moves the text cursor up one line.
↓	Moves the text cursor down one line.
Ctrl+←	Moves the text cursor left one word.
Ctrl+→	Moves the text cursor right one word.
Home	Moves the text cursor to the start of the line.
End	Moves the text cursor to the end of the line.
Delete	Deletes the character immediately to the right of text cursor.
Backspace	Deletes the character immediately preceding text cursor.
PgUp	Moves the text cursor up one screen page.
PgDn	Moves the text cursor down one screen page.
Ctrl+PgUp	Moves the text cursor up one full page in the document.
Ctrl+PgDn	Moves the text cursor down one full page in the document.
Ctrl+↑	Moves the text cursor to the preceding paragraph.
Ctrl+↓	Moves the text cursor to the next paragraph.
Ctrl+Delete	Deletes characters from the cursor's position to the end of the line. (*Note:* This may not work for Windows 95 computers.)
Ctrl+End	Moves the text cursor to the end of the document.
Ctrl+Home	Moves the text cursor to the beginning of the document.

Various keyboard keys

The following keys affect the way the keyboard functions. Often, these keys are used in conjunction with other keys:

✔ **Caps Lock:** The Caps Lock key enables you to type all capital letters without having to hold down the Shift key. Press the Caps Lock key once, and all your letters appear in uppercase; press it again, and the letters you type return to their normal lowercase state. The Caps Lock key affects only letters; pressing a number key with Caps Lock turned on, for example, doesn't cause the symbol above the number to appear.

✔ **Num Lock:** Num Lock makes the numeric keypad on the right side of the keyboard produce numbers. Press this key again, and you can use the arrow keys (displayed on some of the keys in the numeric keypad) to move the text cursor.

✔ **Scroll Lock:** Scroll Lock is sort of a useless key. If you turn it on when you are using certain spreadsheets and then use the arrow keys to move around the document, you find that you can move by row or column instead of by individual cell. So if you're using a spreadsheet and the cursor-control keys seem to be acting funny, check to see if the Scroll Lock light (provided on many keyboards) is illuminated on your keyboard.

✔ **Shift:** Hold down the Shift key before you press a letter key to make a capital letter. You also can insert %, @, #, ^, and so on by typing the number keys while pressing the Shift key.

✔ **Ctrl:** The Control key, labeled Ctrl, is used in combination with another key to carry out specific commands. For example, in many applications you can press the Ctrl key along with the S key (Ctrl+S) to save a file.

✔ **Alt:** Use the Alt key in combination with other keys to carry out commands. For example, press the Alt key and the F4 key (Alt+F4) to close a window on the desktop.

The Caps Lock, Num Lock, and Scroll Lock keys are often represented by lights located (usually) in the upper-right corner of the keyboard. When the light is illuminated for one of these keys, it means that feature is turned on.

Mouse Basics

Using the mouse is an important part of the computer. Many of the commands you use to get things done involve the mouse.

You can do these things with the mouse: click, double-click, right-click, drag, point, and select (or highlight).

✔ **Click:** Press and release the mouse's main button, the one on the left.

✔ **Double-click:** Two quick clicks in a row, both pointing at the same spot.

✔ **Right-click:** Press and release the right button on the mouse.

✔ **Drag:** Move the mouse around while pressing and holding down the main mouse button. In Windows, this technique is used to move objects around on the screen. The drag ends when you release the mouse button.

✔ **Point:** Move the mouse pointer on the screen so that it's hovering over some object, such as a button.

✔ **Select:** Point to something on the screen and then click to highlight it. Sometimes, you need to drag the mouse around or over one or more items to select them.

Clicking the mouse

A click is a single press of the mouse button.

You are likely to read things that say something like "Click the OK button." This instruction means that some type of graphic appears on-screen with the word *OK* on it. Move your mouse (which moves the pointer on the screen) until the pointer is over the word *OK.* Then with your index finger, click the left mouse button. This is referred to as "clicking the mouse." If you need to click the right mouse button instead of the main (left) button, the instructions tell you to "right-click" or to "click the right mouse button." These same instructions are true for the wheel button, if you happen to have an IntelliMouse that includes a little wheel between the other two regular buttons.

When you press the button on your mouse, it makes a clicking noise. So most programs tell you to "click" your mouse button when they mean for you to press it.

Double-clicking the mouse

A double-click is two rapid clicks in a row. You do this in Windows to open a file or a folder. Don't move the mouse around between the clicks — both clicks have to be on the same spot.

Clicking and double-clicking are two different activities. When an instruction tells you to "click," click the left mouse button once. Double-clicking is clicking the left button twice.

If you double-click your mouse and nothing happens, you may not be clicking fast enough. Try clicking it as fast as you can. If this speed is too quick for you, it can be adjusted. *See also* "Mousing Around" later in this section to find out how to adjust your double-click speed.

Dragging the mouse

You drag the mouse when you want to select a group of items on the screen or when you want to move something around on the screen. For example, you can drag the mouse to move your desktop icons to more convenient locations.

Follow these steps to drag something with the mouse:

1. Point the mouse cursor at whatever it is that you want to drag.

2. Press and hold down the left mouse button as you move the
mouse to a new location. The drag operation is really a
move — you start at one point on the screen and move (drag)
the item to another location.

3. Lift your finger to release the mouse button.

You're done dragging. When you release the mouse button, you let
go of whatever it was that you were dragging.

You can also drag to select a group of items. In this case, dragging
draws a rectangle around the items you want to select.

Pointing the mouse

When you're told to "point the mouse," it means that you use the
mouse pointer to point at something on the screen. Don't actually
pick up the mouse and point it at something.

Selecting with the mouse

Selecting is the same as clicking. When you are told to select that
doohickey over there, you move the mouse pointer and click on
the doohickey. Simple.

To deselect something, such as when you click on the wrong thing
or change your mind, just click somewhere else — on the desktop,
for example. That deselects whatever object you clicked.

Sluggish mice

Computer mice begin to slow over time. Sometimes, dirt and muck
get inside the mouse and slow it down. Other times, it's just that
your mouse is wearing out. Whatever the reason, the solution is
fairly simple: Buy another mouse.

Computer mice typically work well for two to three years. After
that, for some reason, they get sluggish and jerky. Rather than
pound your mouse into your desktop, just break down and buy a
new one. You'll be amazed at how much better it works, and how
much more calmly you use your PC.

You can clean your mouse ball with a Q-Tip dipped in rubbing alco-
hol. This can sometimes extend the life of your mouse.

The stuck mouse

You may notice that your mouse is suddenly gone. Then it appears, and then it's gone again. Your mouse is stuck. And honestly, no one knows why this happens. And who really cares why? All you want to know is how to fix it.

The only solution for weird mouse behavior is to reset your computer. *See also* "Resetting Your Computer" in "The Big Picture" section at the front of the book.

Tweaking the mouse in Windows

The Mouse Properties dialog box is where you tweak your mouse — you know, play with all the mouse settings. You can adjust your mouse to accommodate left handers, change the speed of the double-clicking process, or even change the way your mouse pointer looks.

Follow these steps to open the Mouse Properties dialog box:

1. Click the Start button.

2. Choose Settings

3. Choose Control Panel. The Control Panel's main window appears.

Mouse

4. Double-click the mouse icon. The Mouse Properties dialog box opens. Click each tab at the top of the dialog box to check out each section.

5. If you want to make a change to a setting, do so and click OK. If you don't want to mess with anything and you're happy with the way your mouse works, click Cancel and move on.

You see a different dialog box if you have the Microsoft IntelliMouse (the mouse with the wheel) installed on your computer. The dialog box associated with the IntelliMouse has more options and goodies. *See also* "The IntelliMouse" section a little later in this part.

The mouse pad

You need a *mouse pad* to get the best use from your mouse. A mouse pad is a small piece of plastic or rubber that sits on your desk. The best mouse pads have a rough, sort of cloth-like surface that the mouse can really grip. Poorly designed mouse pads are the slick-surfaced type.

Mousing Around

Not every mouse user is right-handed, nor does every computer user sit down and use the mouse with grace and ease. This section helps you to practice your mouse-clicking skills and to change the mouse from being right-handed friendly to left-handed friendly.

The left-handed mouse

If you're one of the southpaws of the world, you can choose to use your mouse on the right side of your computer or the left side, where it may be more intuitive for you. Heck, even some right-handers like a left-handed mouse. But don't go overboard and try to use two mice at once — that's being obsessive.

Follow these steps to make your mouse left-hand friendly:

1. Click the Start button.

2. Choose Settings.

3. Choose Control Panel.

4. Double-click the mouse icon. The Mouse Properties dialog box opens.

5. On the Buttons tab, click to select the option button beside Left-handed. The highlight on the demo mouse shifts from the left button to the right button — which is where you want it to be if you're left-handed.

6. Click OK to close the dialog box.

You've just switched mouse buttons, so from here on, you use the *right* button to click, double-click, and open things. You use the *left* button to make shortcut menus appear. So now when you read, "Right-click on the desktop," you actually click the left button. Remember this!

Practicing the double-click

A great place to practice your double-clicks in Windows is in a special area of the Mouse Properties dialog box. You can double-click on a tiny jack-in-the-box icon there to test your double-clicking skills.

Follow these steps to practice your double-clicking skills:

1. Click the Start button.

2. Choose Settings.

3. Choose Control Panel.

4. Double-click the mouse icon. The Mouse Properties dialog box opens.

5. Click the Buttons tab. Look for the Test area in the lower-right corner.

6. Point the mouse right at the purple jack-in-the-box icon.

7. Click the button twice while you try to keep the mouse steady. It helps if you hold the mouse gently in your hand — if you have a death-grip on the sucker, a double-click will never work. If you're successful, a clown pops up. Egads! Try double-clicking again to put him away.

8. If you find double-clicking difficult, adjust the double-click speed by moving the slider (to the left of the test area) to the Slow end of the scale. Then try double-clicking the jack-in-the-box again.

9. Click OK to close the Mouse Properties dialog box.

The IntelliMouse

Microsoft decided to get into the game of producing mice: thus, the Microsoft IntelliMouse. The *IntelliMouse,* also known as a *wheel mouse,* has a wheel inserted between the two mouse buttons, which enables you to do some neat tricks:

✔ You can roll the wheel up and down to scroll a document (although not all programs respond to the IntelliMouse, so it doesn't always work).

✔ You can press and hold the wheel button to pan the document up, down, left, or right. Quite handy, really.

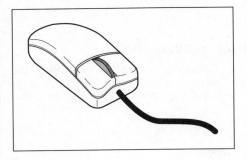

Follow these steps to practice your double-clicking skills with an IntelliMouse:

1. At the far right end of the taskbar, over near where the current time is displayed, double-click the mouse icon (the name *Intellipoint* pops up when you hover your mouse over the icon). The IntelliMouse dialog box opens.

2. Click the Basics tab to bring the panel forward.

3. Double-click the rain clouds at the bottom of the dialog box. This is where you set your double-click rate. The sun goes away and it starts to rain.

4. Double-click the umbrella icon. It should open, indicating that you've passed the test and are no longer getting wet.

5. Click OK to close the Mouse Properties dialog box.

Changing the mouse pointer

Nothing can make someone's jaw drop like seeing a mouse pointer that looks like a pointing hand. "How'd you do that?" they wonder. The trick is a cinch — all you have to do is switch mouse pointers from the boring standard one to something new and different.

Follow these steps to change your mouse pointer:

1. Click the Start button.

2. Choose S̲ettings.

3. Choose C̲ontrol Panel.

4. Double-click the mouse icon. The Mouse Properties dialog box opens.

5. Click the Pointers tab to bring the panel forward. This is where you can choose new mouse pointers to replace the standard ones used in Windows.

6. Click a pointer to change it. For example, click the Busy pointer (the hourglass).

7. Click Browse. This brings up a standard Browse dialog box so that you can hunt down a new pointer. Windows automatically shows you pointers in the Cursors folder (under your Windows folder). If you just downloaded a batch of new cursors from the Internet, browse to the folder you put them in.

8. Double-click a new pointer in the Browse dialog box to select it. If you don't like your new pointer, click the Default button to restore the old pointer.

9. Repeat the steps for each pointer that you want to change. If you really want to make an impact, choose a pointer scheme from the Scheme drop-down list. A *scheme* is merely a preset collection of pointers, all following a particular theme. For example, the Animated Hourglass theme is somewhat interesting.

10. When you finish making changes, click OK. You can click Apply first, if you like. This way, you can try out some of the cursors, but remember, you can always change them later.

Getting Started
with Windows

You must know the basic ingredients to anything you want to build, make, or know. Making cookies? You've got to know that flour and sugar are necessary. Building a house? Lumber and nails are the basics. Using a computer? Microsoft Windows and Help are part of the basics.

In this part . . .

Basic Windows Concepts

In Microsoft Windows, information appears on the screen inside a window. The philosophy behind these windows is that it's easier to manage information when it's displayed inside a contained space, especially when you're working on several things at once. In an environment that uses individual windows, each application runs in its own window without elbowing others out of the way. The control you exercise over these windows is central to how Microsoft Windows works, which is what the following sections are about.

All windows have two basic parts: the frame and the inside. Subtle variations exist among windows in different programs, but certain gizmos are common to all windows and these gizmos work the same way. Knowing what the gizmos are and how to work with them brings you one step closer to feeling in charge of your computer.

Window elements

A typical window includes the following six elements:

Close button

Restore/Maximize button

Minimize button

System menu   Title bar

The purpose of the Lake City Playhouse is to provide quality entertainment for the community of Coeur d'Alene, and the surrounding areas. In addition, Lake City Playhouse is an educational institution. We are the only facility in the North Idaho area that offers theatre education to all ages. We are also the only community theatre in all of North Idaho.

Over the past 37 years, the Lake City Playhouse has experienced growth that has placed it in the forefront of theatre arts in Idaho. Throughout the years, hundreds of volunteers have contributed countless hours in the development of community theatre that enriches the quality of life in our community. Children's workshops and productions are a very important way the Lake City Playhouse has provided opportunities for the cultural development of our community. We believe that community theatre reflects the value of

Window edges

✔ **System menu:** This menu pops open when you click the character at the far left end of the title bar. In Microsoft Word, for
example, that character is a turquoise *W.* The System menu
contains several commands for adjusting the window, but in all
honesty, it's much easier to use your mouse to make these
adjustments. Just in case your mouse is ever broken, however,
you can press Alt+spacebar to open the System menu and then
press the underlined letter in the command you want to use.

✔ **Title bar:** Every window has a name, and the title bar is where
that name is displayed. The title bar is the very top bar on the
screen.

✔ **Minimize button:** You click this button to shrink the window
down to a button on the taskbar, freeing up space on your
screen for other windows. *See also* "The Big Picture" part in this
book to find out more about the Windows taskbar.

✔ **Restore/Maximize button:** The Restore button looks like two
overlapping windows and appears only when a window is maximized. Click it to restore the window to the size it was before
you maximized it. The Maximize button appears when a
window is not full size, as when you have used the Minimize or
Restore button to reduce it. Clicking the Maximize button lets
you zoom the window out until it covers your entire screen,
which is the preferred mode of operation for most windows.

✔ **Close Button:** Click here to make the window go bye-bye. Other
ways to close a window include choosing File⇨Exit (or Quit, or
Close, depending on the application).

✔ **Window edges:** You can "grab" any edge of a window and resize
it by clicking the edge with the mouse and keeping the mouse
button pressed. When a double-headed arrow appears, drag the
edge to the new size that you want. If you drag a window's
corner, you see a diagonal double-headed arrow, which means
that as you drag the window, you are resizing it in two directions at once.

Inside the window

What you see inside a window depends on what the window does.
Regardless of what's going on in the window, however, you most
likely find the following elements:

✔ **Menu bar:** A row of words representing the names of particular
menus that are listed from left to right just under a window's
title bar. Common entries on a menu bar include a File menu,
Edit menu, and Help menu. When you click any of these entries,
a menu of additional choices drops down.

✔ **Toolbars:** A row of buttons, command shortcuts, and other gizmos that generally appear below the menu bar. Many applications offer several different toolbars with buttons for such tasks as formatting, drawing, and working on the Internet.

✔ **Work area:** The open area of the window where all the real work takes place.

✔ **Status bar:** A strip of helpful information about a program, typically located near the bottom of the window. For example, the status bar tells you how complete a backup file is (as in 78% complete).

Adjusting a window

Any time you start an application, its window appears on the screen at some random position and size. Sometimes this is great. Other times you want to rearrange the window's position and size, which is easy to do, if you know how to stretch a window to another size.

Follow these steps to change the size of a window by using the mouse:

1. Point the mouse at the window edge you want to move. When the mouse is positioned correctly, the pointer changes to a vertical or horizontal double-pointed arrow. This arrow shows you which direction you can move the window's edge.

2. Press and hold down the mouse button and then move the mouse left or right to move the edge in that direction, making the window larger or smaller along that one edge.

3. Release the mouse button when you're pleased with the size. The window snaps to the new edge, changing its size.

You can move two of the window's edges at once by pointing at a corner until a diagonal double-pointed arrow appears. When you move this diagonal arrow, the height and width of the window is enlarged or reduced proportionally.

Follow these steps to move two edges at once:

1. Point the mouse at one of the window's corners. Any of the four corners will do, although the most popular corner to grab is the lower right. The mouse pointer changes to a diagonally pointing arrow when it's positioned correctly. Like dragging a window's edge, this shows you which direction you can move.

2. Drag the corner to a new position.

- You can drag the corner in two directions at once, making the window taller and wider or shorter and narrower.

- If you drag the window too small, the menu bar "wraps" itself down to a second or third line. Toolbars also disappear when a window is too narrow.

3. Release the mouse button. The window snaps to its new size.

Some windows may not stretch in the traditional way. If you see a triangle with a ribbed look in the lower-right corner of a window, it's a sign that you can't stretch it as you do a normal window. Often, the only way to change the size on a window of this type is to drag it by the triangle. Generally, you can drag these windows only in one direction or another, or they must maintain a minimum size so that you can see their contents. Note that most status bars have a triangle in their lower-right corner. This may or may not mean that this is the only way to stretch the window.

Maximizing and restoring a window

If you want to resize a window to fill the entire screen, click the Maximize button. This makes the window full-size, no matter the size or shape of your screen. When a window is maximized, you can't stretch the window — it's already stretched to its maximum size — and you can't even see the window's edges.

After clicking on the Maximize button, it changes to another button — the Restore button. This button returns your window to the size and position it was before maximizing.

Moving a window

Moving a window around is as simple as a click-and-drag procedure. But knowing where to click is the secret.

Follow these steps to drag a window:

1. Point the mouse at the window's title bar.

2. Press and hold down the mouse button.

3. Move the mouse — and the window — to a new position. As you drag the mouse on your desktop, an outline of the window on the screen mimics those movements. This outline gives you a rough idea of how your window fits in the place that you're moving it to.

4. Release the mouse button, and the window falls into place.

Finding stray windows

Sometimes a window wanders to the side of the screen, slipping out of mouse reach. When this happens, you may be tempted to just reset your computer. Instead, here's a trick that you can try.

Follow these steps to retrieve a wandering window:

1. Close or minimize any windows on the screen, except for the one that you can't get to. You want your stray window to be the only one open.

2. Open the taskbar's shortcut menu by right-clicking any open spot on the taskbar. If you can't find a blank spot, right-click the current time at the far right. The shortcut menu that opens contains all the vital commands you need; it just includes one additional menu option that you don't see on the basic taskbar shortcut menu.

3. Choose Cascade from the menu. All windows are instantly resized and placed in an overlapping manner in the upper-left corner of the screen. Now you can get at your "lost" window and do your work.

Scrollbars

What you see in a window is merely a small portion of something that can be much bigger. For example, a chapter of the mystery novel that you're writing may be 25 pages long, but you can see only 23 lines or so on the screen at a time. To see the rest of the document, you have to scroll.

You can scroll either up and down or left and right. To control how you scroll and which parts of your document you see, you use a vertical or horizontal scrollbar.

The following figure shows a horizontal scrollbar.

The scrollbar doesn't really move the image on the screen; instead, it moves the window. To see the left side of your document, for example, you might click the left-pointing arrow at the left end of the horizontal scrollbar. Surprisingly, that actually moves the window to the left, causing your document to seem to move to the right. Likewise, clicking the right-pointing arrow on the horizontal scrollbar moves the window to the right, so your document seems to be moving to the left. This confuses some beginners, but you can get used to it before you know it.

The most interesting part of the scrollbar is its elevator box (or thumb tab) — the darker gray shaded box that sits in each scrollbar. This is the box that moves either up or down or left and right. The position of the elevator box in the scrollbar gives you a visual clue about where you are in the document. For example, if the elevator box is at the top of the vertical scrollbar, you know you're looking at the beginning of your document. If it's somewhere near the middle of the scrollbar, you know that what you're viewing falls somewhere towards the middle of the document.

You can also click and drag the elevator box within the scrollbar to scroll more quickly than you can by clicking the arrows on the ends of the scrollbars.

Beginning a Program

Windows is not a program. Windows is more like the brains behind everything that gets the work done. Software is what you actually work with and is considered the program. Starting software in Windows is the first step to working.

Here are the rest of the steps:

1. Click the Start button (located at the bottom left corner of your screen), and a menu opens.

2. Hover the mouse over the word Programs. The Programs submenu opens.

3. Move your mouse pointer into the Programs submenu and hover the mouse over the word Accessories.

4. Move the mouse pointer in the Accessories submenu to hover over one of the options there, such as a game or WordPad.

5. Your program starts, and the Start menu goes away.

There may be times that the program you want to start has been added directly to your Start menu. In that case, it appears in the top section of the main Start menu. If so, you can simply point to it and click to start the program.

These menus can be a bit slippery. One wrong move on your part, and the menu or submenu may disappear. It's not as drastic as it sounds, however; you just have to begin the process over by clicking the Start menu or other entry. Just have a careful hand when messing with those menus and submenus.

If you ever want to close the open Start menus and submenus quickly, click someplace on your screen, outside the open menus, and all the menus close.

Starting your program from an icon on the desktop

The quick-and-dirty way to start a program is to find the program's icon sitting on the desktop. For example, you may see an icon named Internet Explorer, which is a program already pasted on your desktop. Not all programs have an icon on the desktop. The desktop is saved for those special programs that were already there or those programs that you feel are special enough to put there yourself.

Follow these steps to open a program from an icon on the desktop:

1. Find the program on the desktop.

2. Double-click the icon with the mouse.

See also "Setting up a shortcut icon on the desktop" later in this section to find out how to put your favorite program on the desktop.

Starting a program from My Computer

My Computer shows you all the stuff in your computer in the form of icons. You see disk drives, folders, and files. Some of those icons are actually shortcuts to programs, so you simply double-click the icon to start the program.

To tell you the truth, I don't like starting a program from My Computer. I feel that there are easier ways to start a program. In fact, you may find that you use My Computer to start a program only when the program is on a floppy disk or a CD-ROM.

Follow these steps to start a new program in My Computer:

1. Double-click the My Computer icon on your Windows desktop.

2. Double-click Drive (C:).

3. Double-click Program Files.

4. Double-click Accessories.

5. Double-click the program (WordPad, for example).

Setting up a shortcut icon on the desktop

Follow these steps to place an icon for your favorite program on the desktop:

1. Open the Explorer program. You can do this by right-clicking the mouse on the My Computer icon and choosing Explore from the pop-up menu that appears.

2. Browse through Explorer until you locate the program or folder for which you want to create a shortcut. *See also* Part V about finding specific files.

3. Right-click the mouse button and, while holding down the mouse button, drag the program's icon from Explorer to the desktop.

4. Release the right button.

5. Choose Create Shortcut(s) Here from the menu. (You may or may not get this menu. Windows may just give you an automatic shortcut icon without showing you the menu.)

 6. Your icon is placed on the desktop and a shortcut icon appears. Shortcut icons are represented by a little curved arrow in the bottom-left corner of the icon.

Using the Start menu

The Start button, which opens the Start menu, is a good way to find programs because all the programs in your computer are listed on one of the menus or submenus accessed from this button.

Follow these steps to start a program from the Start menu:

1. Click the Start button to open the Start menu.

2. Choose Programs. A submenu opens offering you additional choices.

3. Click one of the programs listed on the Programs submenu. This opens the program, be it Word, Excel, or whatever.

Opening a file to start an application

You're browsing through Windows Explorer, cleaning up some files, when you notice a file called Favorite Songs. Your list of favorite songs! You've just got to visit this one.

Double-click the file and the program that created the file opens. For example, if you created your list of favorite songs in Excel, double-clicking the Favorite Songs file in Explorer automatically opens the Excel program.

See also Part V to find out how to organize your files.

Suppose that you have named a document Proposal, but you can't find it because you don't remember what folder you saved it in. Now's the time to use the Run command.

Follow these steps to open a file by using the Run command:

1. Click the Start button to open the Start menu.

2. Choose Run. The Run dialog box appears.

3. In the text box, type the name of the file you want to open. You use this the most when you install software such as children's games or perhaps a ClipArt package. For example, to install the *Galaxy of Home Office ClipArt,* you are asked to Choose RUN, type D:\SETUP, and then press Enter.

4. Click OK. Windows finds your file and opens it in the program in which you created it.

Getting Help

Microsoft Windows 98 does a pretty good job of helping you find your topic when you're only vaguely sure of what you're asking. Sometimes, knowing the question to ask is the hard part, especially when what you want to ask is, "What is that doohickey that does that blocky thing for you?"

The F1 key — the quick way to get help

The F1 key is designed to give quick answers when you're in an application and need some help. Just press F1 wherever you are, and help pops up.

Sometimes, the F1 key gives you a description or definition of your location, and sometimes you see real information on getting something done.

When you're finished reviewing the information, press the Esc key to return to your document, or click the mouse somewhere on your screen.

The "?"

You may see a little question mark button in the upper-right corner of a dialog box. Clicking this button activates a feature that lets you point and click at anything in the window to get help on it.

After clicking on the ? button, the mouse pointer changes to an arrow with a question mark by it. Then you can click on an item in the window to see a pop-up bubble explaining what the item is or how it works. Click the mouse again (or press the Esc key) to make the bubble go away.

Windows Help system

Windows has its own Help system that you can access directly and that is designed to support you when you're looking for information. Windows Help offers several ways to get help: a table of contents, an index, and a full-text search feature.

Follow these steps to open the Windows Help system:

1. Click the Start button.

2. Click Help, and you see the following tabs:

   - **Contents tab:** The Contents tab is organized as a table of contents. To open a category, double-click its name. This displays a list of topics in that category. To open a topic, double-click its name. This opens a separate window that details information about the topic, often including step-by-step instructions. To close a category, and make the screen a little more readable, double-click its name again.

   - **Index tab:** All information about a specific topic is organized in the index. You can use the index to find a topic if you know exactly what it is. If you know something about what you want help with, such as bold text, type the word **bold.** The information comes up. Click the Display button, and the information appears on the right side of your screen.

   - **Search tab:** Type a keyword in the box at the top of the panel that best describes the topic you are searching for. Your keyword may bring up several topics, which may have several subtopics.

3. Click Display. The information is displayed for you to preview.

Getting outside help

Pressing the F1 key or going into the Windows Help System isn't always going to get you the answers that you need. Sorry to break that news to you, but it's true. Sometimes, you have to actually break down and talk to a person — a real, breathing person who asks you questions.

Follow these suggestions for making the most of the time you spend talking to live persons for help:

- ✔ **A computer guru:** A computer guru is someone who loves computers and knows enough about them to offer help when you need it. Don't make me your computer guru. Find someone at work or school or even a family member who can answer your questions.

Your computer guru at work is probably the computer manager or systems administrator. But ask around because it may be the mail room clerk who's a secret computer genius.

✓ **Computer consultants:** A computer consultant is someone who likes computers and charges you a fee for information. Consultants help you get out of trouble, offer suggestions, buy things for you, set up your system, train you about software, and create custom programs, but they do charge a fee. And this fee can get costly, especially when the answer to a question may be as simple as turning your monitor on or plugging in a phone cord.

✓ **Computer stores:** Some computer stores may offer classes or have special store personnel responsible for answering questions. Depending on the store, this may be a limited source of information.

✓ **Computer clubs:** Computer clubs are popping up all over the place. The best place to find these clubs is from a listing in your local paper, from a computer flyer, or in a local computer newspaper or magazine. You can also check with local colleges to see if they have campus computer clubs.

✓ **Community colleges:** Community colleges offer introductory courses on computers and some software programs. Come equipped with your questions.

✓ **Technical support people:** The technical support people at your computer store and the telephone support you get with every piece of software you buy are always available to answer questions. Be prepared to sit on the phone and wait. Calling technical support is never a quick answer, and you may have to wait on hold before you actually get to speak to a person. Have your computer information ready, too. You may need software registration numbers and the like.

✓ **Internet:** Don't overlook searching for help on the Internet. Microsoft has its own tech support web page at www.microsoft.com. Type the words **technical support** in the Search box for all kinds of information.

✓ **Newsgroups:** You can find newsgroups for just about every subject. Don't overlook these online discussion groups — they are a great way to share information. Find a newsgroup relating to the software that you have a question about and see if you can't find another participant in the group who has the solution.

Hardware or software problems

A lot of hardware problems can be fixed by checking cables, listening for noises, watching for sparks, and so on. And software problems are usually cured by a friend or by technical support. But how do you know whether your problem is one of hardware or software?

Use this list of clues to begin your evaluation:

- **Does the problem happen regardless of which program you're running?** For example, do WordPad, Excel, and Quicken all refuse to send stuff to the printer? If so, it's a hardware problem. Specifically, the printer is not working properly. Check the power. Check the cables. Check the printer.

- **Did the problem just crop up?** For example, did Print Preview work yesterday but not today? If so, it could be a hardware problem, it could be a network problem, or it could be a software driver problem — provided that nothing has been changed on your computer and no new software has been added since the last time the program worked properly.

- **Does the problem happen with only one application?** For example, does the computer always reset when you try to print using your photo editor? If so, it's a software problem. Call the developer.

Very generally speaking, if the problem happens in only one program, it's software. If the problem occurs throughout all your applications or at random times, it's hardware.

Calling tech support

Tech support is not what it once was. In the old days, you could call an 800 number for free help. Occasionally, you can still find this kind of free help, but it's not very common anymore. Now you usually have to "pay as you go" for tech support or it's simply nonexistent. Before you call tech support, try to find out how much it's going to cost you. You don't want to be surprised with an enormous bill. And try visiting the company's Web page before you dial that phone. Look for support information or a FAQ (Frequently Asked Questions) page. You may find your answer there.

These helpful hints may make your life easier if you do find that you must call tech support:

- **Know your hardware.** Know how much memory is installed, the name and number of the microprocessor, the type or brand name of the computer, and the serial number of the device.

✔ **Have your information handy.** Tech support needs to know the serial number, version number, and maybe a registration number for any software problems. I think part of the reason that they ask for this information is to ensure that they aren't giving you technical support on stolen software.

✔ **Know the problem well enough that you are able to reproduce the problem.**

✔ **Be prepared to take advice, no matter how simple the answer might seem.** Tech support people are sometimes frustrated by people who ask questions but refuse to take the answer because the solution is too simple.

✔ **Write down the solution.** That way, you don't have to phone tech support again for the same problem.

✔ **Don't waste the tech support person's time by asking simple questions.** Check Web sites and Windows Help first so that you don't take up their time with basic questions. Save these tech folks for the really mind-boggling problems.

✔ **Try reading the manual.** Now there's a concept! Check out the documentation that came with the software, or pick up one of the fine computer books written by yours truly, Dan and Sandy Gookin.

Multitasking

The fun part of Windows is the ability to run several programs at one time. Consider it high-tech juggling. This process of running several programs at once is known as *multitasking*. The concept behind multitasking is that you don't have to quit one program to start another — you just keep switching back and forth.

You multitask when you play a game of FreeCell, run the Word program, play a CD on your computer stereo, and download an MP3 file from a Web site — all at the same time!

Why is this important? This multitasking capability enables you to print your 150 personalized Christmas letters while catching up on your e-mail. Or you can view two different Web pages at a time. Or you can play a game and then quickly switch back to your word processor when your supervisor wanders by. All this is called multitasking.

See also "Switching between Programs" later in this part.

The Quick Launch Bar

One of the handy toolbars that Windows offers is the Quick Launch bar. The true joy behind the Quick Launch bar is its "one click to start a program" feature.

Follow these steps to display the Quick Launch bar:

1. Right-click the taskbar. You must click on an empty spot on the taskbar or you get a different menu. So don't click on any icon already on the taskbar.

2. Choose Toolbars.

3. Choose Quick Launch from the pop-up menu.

Follow these steps to add new icons to the Quick Launch bar:

1. Right-click My Computer.

2. Choose Explore.

3. Find the program that you want to add to the Quick Launch Bar.

4. Click and drag the icon to the Quick Launch Bar.

Tah-dah! Your new program icon is now happily situated in the Quick Launch Bar.

Follow these steps to see the Quick Launch bar displayed with large icons:

1. Right-click the Quick Launch bar.

2. Choose View.

3. Choose Large from the pop-up menu.

 Put only the really important or frequently used programs on the Quick Launch bar. It defeats the purpose of being quick and helpful if you put everything there.

Quitting a Program

When you're finished working, quit your program and wander off to do something else. This command is perhaps the best one of any Windows program.

Follow these steps to quit something:

1. Choose File from the menu bar at the top of the screen.

2. Choose Exit from the list of options.

Don't be confused if your program doesn't seem to have a File menu or an Exit command. If you can't find either one, look for the last command at the bottom of the first menu. That typically is the one you can use to quit a program. Alternatively, you can click the program's Close button (the X) in the upper-right corner of the window.

Shortcuts

Most folks use the same documents over and over: Travel Reports, To Do lists, incessant projects left unfinished, and so on. To access these documents easily, you can make a shortcut to the report or to the folder holding the report. You can then put this shortcut on your desktop — essentially you make the file or folder a desktop icon. That way, when you want to go directly to the file called Bora Bora, you can click the shortcut to that file and it opens immediately — no more going through the long process of opening up a program and searching for the file.

Follow these steps to stick a shortcut icon on your desktop:

1. Right-click My Computer and choose Explore from the pop-up menu.

2. Browse until you find the program or file for which you want to make the shortcut. You may have to do some searching and click through some different drives or folders to find just exactly what you're looking for.

3. Click once on the program or file to highlight it.

4. Choose File⇨Create Shortcut. This creates a shortcut icon.

5. Click and drag the shortcut icon to the desktop.

Obviously, different people work on different projects, but here are some popular shortcut items that tend to rest on many desktops:

✔ Internet Explorer (or a similar Internet software program)

✔ Word processing programs, such as Microsoft Word

✔ Current projects that you may have to visit on a daily basis

✔ General work tools, such as a calculator or a game

Switching between Programs

Switching between programs is simply for those overly ambitious people who think they can do more than one thing at once. Well, yes, your computer is capable of doing several things at once, but you're limited to doing only one thing at a time. But this ability to switch between several programs, all running at the same time, makes you feel that you're getting lots done.

Use these options for switching to another program:

✔ **Option 1:** Grab the mouse and click on another program's window. This works only as long as that window is visible. Clicking on a window brings that window to the front of the screen (so to speak).

✔ **Option 2:** If you can't see the window to any other programs (probably because your current program is taking up all the screen space), look for a button on the taskbar that corresponds to the window you want. Click that button, and the window comes forward.

✔ **Option 3:** Shrink the current window by clicking the minimize button, which is located in the upper-right corner of the window.

✔ **Option 4:** Use the Alt+Tab key combination. Press Alt and then press and release Tab while still holding down the Alt key. A box opens in the middle of your screen that displays all programs that you currently have open (as represented by a button on the taskbar). As you continue to hold down the Alt key, press and release the Tab key to toggle through all open programs. When the box shows the name of the program that you want to switch to, release the Alt key and that program appears on-screen.

✔ **Option 5:** Use the Alt+Esc key combination. Press and hold down Alt and then press Esc. Release both keys. This switches you to the next active program you have open. The programs show up in the order in which you opened them (which also happens to be the order in which their buttons are displayed on the taskbar). You may have to keep pressing the Alt+Esc combination a few times to find the program or window that you want.

Ways to Start Your Computer

Starting a computer is easy. Getting it to do what you want is the problem. But to make starting a computer more difficult, the computer whizzes out there have come up with a whole group of terms, each of which really means "start the computer." Take a look at this sampling:

Term	Translation
Power up	This is the geek term for turning on the computer.
Power on	This means the same thing as power-up.
Boot	This refers specifically to starting your computer's operating system.
Reset	This interrupts the computer from whatever it's doing and forces it to start all over (a warm boot).
Warm boot	This is another term for resetting the computer; everything starts over with the power still on.
Reboot	This just means the same thing as reset or warm boot.
Cold boot	This means to restart equipment that has been turned off. Also known as a *cold start*.

Work Commands

After you learn one Windows program, like Word or Notepad, learning the rest isn't hard. Most Windows programs do things pretty much the same way. For example, after you learn how to copy, cut, and paste text, you can do these functions in just about any Windows application. And you can use copy, cut, and paste on more than just text. The same process also applies to files, folders, and most graphics, too. Pretty nifty stuff, huh?

Copy

To copy text, files, folders, or whatever you want in Windows, follow these steps:

1. Select what you want to copy with the mouse. Do this by dragging the mouse over some text, clicking a picture or an icon with the mouse, or dragging the mouse around the object. This highlights the text, picture, or icon, which means that it has been selected and is ready for copying.

2. Choose Edit.

3. Choose Copy.

The information you are copying is placed on what is known as a *Clipboard*. It's like a holding tank for information that has been either copied or cut until you're ready to place it somewhere else.

The shortcut step for copying anything is to select the text, file, folder or whatever, and then press Ctrl+C. Now, your text or picture is ready to be pasted either into the same program or another program.

Cut

To cut something from a program is to delete it. Remember that when you cut anything from a program, it removes it completely. It's almost as if you cut a nice picture of a diamond out of a magazine — that picture is gone.

Follow these steps to cut a picture, text — or whatever:

1. Select a picture, text, or an icon.

2. Choose Edit.

3. Choose Cut. The picture or text you cut is now copied to the Clipboard and is deleted from your application.

If you want to paste the information that you cut before a file, be sure to do so before you use the Cut or Copy command again. When you place new text on the Clipboard by cutting or copying again, it overwrites the first text you placed there. *Remember:* After you cut something from a document, it's gone for good.

The shortcut for cutting something is Ctrl+X.

Paste

You use the Paste command to take whatever you stored on the Clipboard (by using the Cut or Copy command) — text, picture, file, folder, whatever — and place it into a program.

Follow these steps to paste something that you have already cut or copied:

1. Position your cursor on the screen where you want to paste the cut or copied material.

2. Choose Edit.

3. Choose Paste.

You can paste material cut or copied from any Windows application into another Windows application.

The shortcut for pasting is Ctrl+V.

Pasting does have a few rules. You cannot paste graphics into a program that cannot accept graphics, and you cannot paste text into a program that works only with graphics.

Open

You can use the Open command to retrieve anything that you have saved to your hard drive.

Follow these steps to open a file:

1. Choose File.

2. Choose Open. The Open dialog box appears.

3. Browse to the file that you want to open and click it once to highlight it.

4. Click the Open button.

Print

You use the Print command to take the lovely work that you see on-screen and print it onto paper.

Follow these steps to send something on your screen to the printer:

1. Choose File.

2. Choose Print. The Print dialog box appears, which has a bunch of hocus-pocus in it.

3. From the Name drop-down list, choose the name of the printer that you want to send your document to.

4. Click OK.

Here are some tips to help you print a good hard copy of your work:

- Check that the printer is turned on and is on-line and ready to print.

- Be sure that the printer has paper.

- In the Print dialog box, make sure that you have indicated the number of copies and which pages you want to print if you aren't printing the entire document.

Save

If you've finished cutting and copying and pasting and all those glorious things to make your text just perfect, it's time to save your work.

Follow these steps to save your work:

1. Choose File.

2. Choose Save. The Save As dialog box appears.

3. Type the name of your file in the File Name text box.

4. Click the Save button.

You must give your document a name and tell Windows where to store it the first time you save it. After that, you can just click the Save button on the toolbar to continue saving your work with that same filename and to the same location. Just remember to save! In fact, get into the habit of saving every five minutes or so — just to be safe. That way, if your computer freezes up and you have to restart it, you won't have that much of your work to re-create. **See also** Part VI to find out more about saving your work.

The shortcut command for saving your file is Ctrl+S. Be sure to save your work every 5 to 10 minutes. If you don't save, your computer won't remember all that hard work you've done. If your computer suddenly freezes up and you have to reset, all that unsaved information is lost. Get in the habit of reaching your mouse up and clicking the Save icon — it looks like a floppy disk.

Undo

We, as humans, can be sloppy. And sometimes this sloppiness spills over into our work in Windows. The answer to your sloppiness is the Undo command. This command undoes whatever foolish thing you just did.

To undo something, choose Edit⇨Undo. Undo works on just about anything, such as replacing cut graphics or text.

The shortcut command for Undo is Ctrl+Z.

The following figure illustrates the shortcut keys for some very important tasks: Undo, Cut, Copy, and Paste. Press the Ctrl key plus Z, X, C, or V, respectively.

Redo

The Redo key (as in re-Do that move again) is for those people that can't make up their minds or who are extremely klutzy with their keyboard and mouse.

Let's say you delete a line of text. Oops, you didn't want to do that so you follow the above steps for the Undo command (or simply click on the Undo button on the toolbar). This puts that line of text back into your document. But then you decide that little deletion error really works well so you want to redo what you just did (which in this case would be to delete the line of text again).

Redo can be accomplished by choosing Edit⇨Redo (this is the second line down — redo or repeat or some words that describe what you're wanting — but it's the second line down). Or you can click the redo button on the taskbar. It's the arrow swinging to your right.

Dealing with Disk Drives

Windows has an abundance of jobs. One of these many jobs is to manage information that you collect in your computer. You may accumulate tons of documents and images in your computer. Much of the information is useful and some is not so useful — for example, the endless stream of bad jokes you receive through e-mail, that novel you keep trying to finish, and pictures of your friends' kids. Your PC probably has at least three types of disk drives, possibly more. Disk drives are used for storing stuff — the operating system, programs, and all the many wonderful things you create on your PC. This part tells you how to work with those disk drives in Windows.

In this part . . .

Figuring Out Which Drive Is Which

Why bother having disk drives? I mean, the computer has memory (RAM), right? Many PCs are sold with 32, 64, or more megabytes of RAM. That seems to be enough, so why even bother with this disk storage stuff?

 A megabyte is a million bytes, or enough storage space to hold one million characters, one thousand pages of information, or several hundred graphics files. That's a lot of space.

The reason you should bother with disk storage is that disk drives are for long-term storage. It's additional storage to the RAM inside your computer. That memory, which is often called temporary memory, is used when you're running a program and creating a document, for example. Computers "think" in RAM.

When you finish creating, you can save your work by making a permanent copy on a disk (either your hard drive or a floppy disk — it doesn't really matter). That's long-term storage, also called permanent storage.

RAM is temporary storage because that memory is erased each time you turn the computer's power off. But if you save your information to a disk, it's available the next time you turn your computer on.

Finding Your Disk Drives

Windows keeps a representation of all your PC's disk drives in the My Computer window.

In order to see all the disk drives on your computer, double-click the My Computer icon on the desktop. The My Computer window pops up and lists all the disk drives in your computer system.

You should be able to locate the following disk drives in the My Computer window:

3½ Floppy (A:)

✔ **Drive A:** Your PC's main floppy disk drive. You manually insert and remove the floppy disk here.

(C:)

✔ **Drive C:** Your PC's main hard disk drive. You may also have a hard drive D and possibly even a hard drive E.

(R:)

✔ **CD-ROM drive:** On most PCs, the CD-ROM or DVD drive is usually given the letter following the last hard drive, which is usually drive D. Even if it's a different letter on your PC, it uses the same icon.

Zip 100 (Z:)

✔ **Other drives:** Other drives may exist in your system, such as the Zip drive (drive Z). A Zip disk is similar to a floppy disk drive but provides more storage capacity. A Zip disk is also physically thicker than a floppy disk, which is why it needs its own drive.

As you can see in the My Computer window, each disk drive has an icon, a letter, and an optional name. The icon indicates which type of disk drive it is: hard disk, floppy disk, or CD-ROM/DVD. My Computer even offers a generic looking icon for removable disks (such as a Zip disk or Magnito Optical disk) — 5¼-inch floppy disks, RAM drives, network drives, and other interesting storage devices.

The CD-ROM, DVD, CD-R, and CD-RW drives all use the same CD-ROM drive icon, but you can change the optional name. *See also* "Naming your disk drives" later in this part to find out how to change the optional name, and see Part XI for more information about CD-R and CD-RW.

The little hand holding a drive indicates that those drives are being shared on a computer network.

Any drives you see with a pipe beneath them are disk drives on network computers. These disk drives are accessed like other drives on your PC, although they exist on other computers on the network.

Drive letters

Disk drives are known by letters, from A (skipping B), C, D, and up to Z. This is how the drives are known to Windows and to your software. Drives A and C are special. Drive A is the first floppy drive — meaning the main floppy drive. Drive C is the first hard drive.

Drive B is reserved for the second floppy drive. Back in the early days when hard drives were outrageously expensive, most PCs were sold without them. The second floppy drive served as a cheap form of extra storage. Today, it's not needed, but letter B is still set aside just in case.

Drive letters are up for grabs after drive C. For example, no hard and fast rule says that drive D must be the CD-ROM drive. If you have any extra hard drives in your PC, they're given drive letters D and up. After the last hard drive letter comes your CD-ROM or DVD drive. This could be drive D or E or anything up to Z.

Because all these drives are up for grabs, you can never count on anything being identical from PC to PC. For this reason, software instructions may say, "Insert the CD into your CD-ROM drive, which may be drive D or drive E" or even ". . . which may be drive *n*, where *n* is the letter of your CD-ROM drive."

Remember: Don't depend on the CD-ROM drive having the same drive letter on every computer!

Naming your disk drives

The hard drives in your PC can each be given a name. You don't have to do this unless you want to see the name displayed in the My Computer window (and other places in Windows). But if you're curious, or if you want to change the name from MICRON or PRESSARIO to something more personal, you can do so.

Follow these steps to change the name of your hard drive:

1. Double-click the My Computer icon located on the desktop.

2. Right-click the disk drive's icon. A pop-up shortcut menu appears.

3. Choose the Properties command from the shortcut menu. This displays the disk drive's Properties dialog box.

4. In the General tab of the dialog box, type the new name for your hard drive in the text box that says Label.

5. Click the OK button to close the dialog box.

Floppy Disk Drive Basics

A floppy disk is a flat, 3½-inch square "coaster" on which you can store about 1.5 megabytes of information. Many programs still come on floppy disks. For example, driver files for new hardware you may add to your PC often come on floppy disks. You can also use floppy disks to move files between two computers. (You can't move extremely large files, but most document files can fit on a floppy disk.)

The most important thing to remember about using your floppy drive is to put a formatted floppy disk into it before you do anything. *See also* "Formatting floppies" later in this part.

In and out goes the floppy disk

To use the floppy disk, you must insert it into your PC's floppy drive.

To properly insert the floppy disk, stick it into the drive, label side up, round metal circle on the bottom, with the shiny metal piece going in first. The disk makes a *thunk* noise when it's in place.

Don't use sticky notes as disk labels! They fall off when you're not looking and can sometimes get stuck inside your disk drives.

To remove the floppy disk, push the button beneath and slightly to the right-of-center of the floppy drive slot. This ejects the disk out of the drive about an inch or so. Grab the disk and put it away.

Always make sure that the computer is not "writing to" the floppy disk before you eject it (the blinking access light on the floppy drive should be off). Also, make sure that you're not currently using any files on the floppy drive; before you eject the disk, close any files that you may have accessed. If you don't, Windows asks you to reinsert the floppy disk so that it can finish writing information.

Formatting floppies

A floppy disk must be formatted before you can use it. Unless you were smart enough to buy preformatted floppy disks, you have to format them at some point. Most computer stores, however, stock preformatted disks. Read the labels carefully to find them — it'll save you some work.

If the disk isn't formatted and you try to access it, Windows spits up an error message. If you get this error message, click the Yes button and get ready to format.

Follow these steps to format a floppy disk:

1. Insert an unformatted disk in drive A. You can stick a brand new disk or a disk you've used before into the drive. If you use an old disk, however, be aware that formatting erases everything on the disk. This could be a devastating act, so be careful.

2. Double-click the My Computer icon.

3. Click once on the icon for drive A.

4. Choose File from the menu bar.

5. Choose Format. The Format dialog box appears.

6. Click the Start button. Windows takes a few minutes to finish formatting. When it finishes, you may or may not see a summary screen. Press Esc to close the dialog box, and you're ready to use the freshly formatted disk.

The A drive

The A drive is your computer's first floppy drive (remember that *first* floppy drive means *main* floppy drive). If you have only one floppy drive, it's the A drive. If you have two floppy drives, Drive A may be either the top or the bottom floppy drive. If you have more than one floppy drive, the second may actually be a Zip drive. (*See also* "Using a Zip Drive" later in this part.) You need to know where your A drive is because software and computer manuals refer to it often.

To find out which floppy drive is which, watch them when your PC starts up. The first floppy drive, Drive A, has a light on it that lights up for a few moments after the PC starts. Immediately write *Drive A* beside that drive using an indelible marker, or use a label maker to create a label for the drive.

Sending a file to drive A

You can send a file to a floppy disk in two ways:

✔ **Option 1:** Choose Drive A from any Save As or Open dialog box.

✔ **Option 2:** Find and select the file (or group of files) that you want to save to drive A. Choose File⇨Send To⇨3½ Floppy (A) from the menu. Don't forget to put a formatted floppy disk into drive A before you do this!

To copy files *from* drive A, open drive A in the My Computer window. Drag or select and copy the files that you want to put somewhere else. *See also* Part VI for more information on working with files.

How Much Space Is on the Disk Drive?

Disk drives fill up, and at some point, you may want to see how much space is available on the disk drive.

Follow these steps to find out how much space is available on a disk drive:

1. Double-click the My Computer icon located on the Desktop.

2. Right-click a disk drive. A disk must be in the floppy drive or CD-ROM drive before you right-click. A pop-up menu appears. *See also* Part II if you need help with right clicking.

3. Choose Properties.

4. Read the General tab area. The amounts of space *used* and *free* for that disk are listed in the General tab area.

5. Click OK to close the dialog box. Don't be surprised if disks such as CD-ROMs and DVDs are always full. These disks can only be read from, not written to.

Remember: You can click the Disk Cleanup button if your disk looks full — when your disk space is represented by only a small slice of the purple pie graphic. *See also* Part X for information on maintaining your computer.

Inserting a CD-ROM or DVD

A CD-ROM drive uses special CD-ROM discs called CDs. Computer CDs look exactly like music CDs, but computer CDs store megabytes of computer information. The CD-ROM drive accesses that information, making it available to you just like it is on a hard disk or a floppy. You can also play music CDs in your computer's CD-ROM drive.

The *RO* in CD-ROM means *Read Only*, which indicates that you can only read information from a CD-ROM disc. You can't add new information to the disc or erase or change information that's already on the disc. Ditto for DVD disks: They're also read-only.

A DVD (Digital Video Disk) drive, also called a *DVD-ROM* drive, looks and acts just like a CD-ROM drive. But in addition to reading computer CDs and music CDs, the DVD drive accesses computer DVD and video DVD disks.

Computer CDs go into CD-ROM drives in one of three ways: caddy, slide-in, or tray. The caddy method is used only by older CD-ROM drives. DVD drives use either the slide-in or tray method. The following list explains how each type works:

- **Caddy:** The disc goes into the caddy with the label up, so you can see the label through the caddy's clear cover. Close the caddy, and shove it into the drive. I don't recommend this type of drive because putting the CD-ROM in the caddy is an unnecessary step to this process.

- **Slide-in:** Slide the CD into the CD-ROM drive — just as you would slide a CD into your car's CD player.

- **Tray:** Press the CD-ROM drive's eject button to pop the tray out of the CD-ROM drive. Drop the CD into the tray, with the label up. Press the CD-ROM drive's eject button again, and the tray slides back into the computer.

Using a Zip Drive

Zip drives are becoming popular alternatives and supplements to the traditional PC floppy disk. You can store 100MB or 250MB of information on a single Zip disk, depending on which model of Zip drive you have. That's nearly 100 or 250 times the capacity of a little old floppy disk.

Zip drives come with many new PCs and are available as options on others. You can add a Zip drive to your PC at any time. Some models are installed internally, whereas others can be attached to your PC with a cable.

Zip disks are available in two formats: 100MB and 250MB. You must have a 250MB Zip drive to read 250MB disks. The 250MB Zip drive can also read 100MB disks, but the 100MB drives can read only 100MB disks.

Zip disks are a great way to transfer massive files from one computer to another.

Inserting a Zip disk

You insert a Zip disk into a Zip drive just as you would insert a floppy disk into a floppy drive — label up with the shiny metal part stuck in first. When you insert a Zip disk, don't force it into the drive. If it doesn't fit, you are probably trying to put the disk in the wrong drive.

Instead of forcing the Zip disk into the drive, carefully push the disk all the way into it. After a certain point, the disk locks into place. At that point, stop pushing it — it's been successfully inserted into your drive, and a Zip disk icon should appear in the My Computer window.

Remember: The Zip disk must be in the drive before you can read or write information to it.

Looking at the Zip menu

After a Zip disk is inserted into the drive, right-click the Zip disk icon in the My Computer window to display a detailed menu with special Zip menu options, as shown in the following figure.

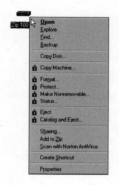

Special commands are flagged by the I (for Iomega, the Zip drive's manufacturer). These are Zip-drive only commands. For example, the Format command is particular to Zip drives. Also notice the Eject command, which you can use to eject a Zip disk automatically. Other commands on the menu are explained in the Zip manual. If you want to learn about more commands, the manual is an excellent resource.

Organizing Your Folders

Organized people are happy people. Ever notice that? Sure! If you know that your scissors are always in the top-left drawer of the kitchen cabinet, you're happy that you can easily find the scissors. But if your children keep moving the scissors, your life quickly becomes miserable because you can't find them. You spend 20 minutes opening every drawer and cabinet to find those darned scissors.

And you can extend this organization to your computer by setting up a logical folder system for storing your files. Without folders, files tend to get scattered around your hard drive, and you may have problems finding them when you need them. By using folders, you can keep similar files together, tucked neatly into a folder labeled appropriately. You can organize your documents by project, by type of file, or by whatever category works for you.

In this part . . .

About Folders

A folder is a storage place for files in your computer's hard drive. Folders keep files together in a neat and easy-to-access place so that you can find them when you need them.

Folders can hold, in addition to files, more folders. It's just another level of organization. For example, a folder called Finances may contain two other folders — one for 1999 and one for 2000. Within the folder for each year, you could store a file showing a list of your investments for that year.

All files on your hard drive are actually stored in a folder. When you save something in Windows, you're really placing it in a specific folder on your hard drive.

Remember: The key is organization. Put files into folders that *you* create for specific purposes, name your folders so that it's easy to figure out what's in each one, and delete unnecessary folders. But be sure that you only delete the unnecessary folders that *you* created. Never delete a folder that you didn't create, or you could delete essential system files by mistake.

Creating a Folder

Creating a folder is easy. Deciding where to create the folder (in other words, organizing) can be a challenge.

Follow these steps to create a folder called Stuff in the My Documents folder on drive C:

1. Double-click the My Documents icon on the desktop.

2. Choose File.

3. Choose New.

4. Choose Folder. A folder named New Folder appears, and the name is highlighted so that you can type a meaningful name.

5. Type a new name for the folder. Be descriptive when naming folders. Remember that this folder may contain files and possibly other folders, all of which should relate somehow to the folder's name so that you can find them again easily. If you can't think of anything for this example, just type the name **Stuff**.

6. Press Enter to lock in the name. The new folder is ready and waiting for you to place new and interesting files into it.

When you're ready to copy files into your new folder, double-click the new folder's icon to open it. For now, a blank window is displayed because it's a new folder and doesn't contain any files yet.

If you don't have a My Documents icon on the desktop (as is probably the case if you're using Windows 95), you can open the My Documents folder by double-clicking the My Computer icon, double-clicking the drive C icon, and then double-clicking the My Documents folder. From there, you can follow the preceding steps, beginning with Step 2.

As you become more organized and involved with more projects, you may want to make more folders and move appropriate files into those new folders. Making folders is an ongoing process of organization.

Deleting a Folder

When you find that you no longer need a particular folder, you can simply throw the folder away, otherwise known as *deleting* the folder.

Follow these steps to delete a folder:

1. Find the folder that you want to trash by using either Windows Explorer or My Computer.

2. Drag the folder that you want to delete across the desktop and drop it on top of the Recycle Bin icon. A warning box may appear, telling you that you're about to delete a folder. The warning box asks if you are sure that you want to delete the folder.

Recycle Bin

3. Click Yes to trash the folder.

You can use the Undo command to immediately undelete a folder that you just trashed (the Undo command undoes your last action, which was deleting the folder). This command only works *immediately* after the folder is deleted, so you can't do anything else and then try to undo; the Undo command won't work.

Follow these steps to undo a deletion:

1. In either My Computer or Windows Explorer, choose <u>E</u>dit.

2. Choose <u>U</u>ndo Delete from the list of options.

You can also press Ctrl+Z, or click the Undo button on the toolbar to undo any action.

Explorer Window

The whole mess of folders on your hard drive is organized into a *tree structure* — much like a family tree. The folders start at the root, branch out to more folders, and eventually end in files — kind of like the leaves on a tree. The Windows Explorer program can help you visualize this tree structure.

Follow these steps to start Windows Explorer:

1. Click the Start button.

2. Choose Programs.

3. Choose Windows Explorer. The Explorer Window opens.

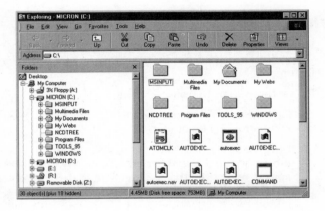

The Explorer window is divided into two parts, or panels. On the left is the tree structure. This is the way your hard drive is organized — from the desktop down to the folders and files. On the right you can see the contents of the folder you selected on the left.

Opening and closing the tree structure

To open a drive or folder in the left panel and display the folders within, you can click the plus sign (+) beside that drive or folder. A "branch" of the tree structure is displayed in the left panel and the plus sign changes to a minus sign, but the display in the right panel of Explorer doesn't change. You can close that branch of the tree structure by clicking the minus sign (–). All subfolders close up into their main folders.

When you finish with Explorer, close its window by clicking the little X (the Close button) in the upper-right corner.

The Explorer toolbar

If you don't see a toolbar across the top of your Explorer screen, choose View⇨Toolbars⇨Standard Buttons. You may also want to choose Address Bar and Text Labels from the Toolbars submenu.

My Computer

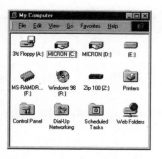

My Computer is an icon on your desktop that, when clicked, opens a window that displays all the stuff you have stored in your computer. My Computer is a visual representation of your computer's hard drives, folders, and files, and it shows you how and where information is stored. Using My Computer is one way to find and organize your folders and files.

The My Computer icon is stuck on the desktop. You can move it around or rename it, but you cannot delete it. Just about everything else on the desktop, however, can be deleted.

Opening My Computer

Open My Computer by double-clicking the icon. Go ahead, double-click and see what happens. A window appears that shows certain goodies lurking inside your computer, similar to what you see in the following figure.

At this stage, you see two types of items: disk drives and special folders. The disk drives represent your computer's disk drives, and the special folders hold other things.

The shape and appearance of the disk drives in My Computer depend on what types of disk drives live inside or nearby. Disk drives, no matter what type, are given letters, and some are also given names. The letters are followed by colons, and they appear in parentheses.

The Control Panel and Printers folders are included in My Computer because they are important parts of your computer, just like the disk drives.

You also see a Dial-Up Networking file (if you're connected to a network) and a Scheduled Tasks folder.

If one of your drives is *shared,* which means that it's connected to a network and other users have been given access to it, you see a serving hand symbol under the icon for that disk drive. Likewise, a drive with a kind of pipe symbol that makes it look like it's connected to a sewer system indicates a drive on someone else's computer on the network, one that your computer is currently "borrowing."

Opening stuff

My Computer displays the goodies inside your computer as icons. To see what's inside an icon — a disk drive, folder, or whatever — you double-click the icon, just as you double-clicked My Computer to open it.

Clicking an icon displays a window that details what the icon represents. When you open a disk drive icon in My Computer, a window appears, displaying folders and files on that disk drive.

Closing stuff

To close a window in Windows, click the Close button (the X in the upper-right corner).

 Clicking the Close button closes the window and removes it from the screen. In case you're wondering, closing a window does not delete the contents of the window. It simply removes the window from view.

You can close windows in any order, no matter which one you opened first.

The stuff inside My Computer

The main My Computer window contains three different items: disk drives, folders, and files. The basic storage container for information on a computer is the *file*. All computer programs are files, and you store your work in files. Everything is organized and represented by an appropriate icon inside My Computer.

Files and folders are stored on various disk drives inside your computer. Those disk drives appear as icons inside the main My Computer window.

To see what files or folders lurk on your disk drives, double-click a disk drive icon to open it. A window appears and details the contents of the disk drive, which is a bunch of folders and files.

Looking at stuff in My Computer

You can adjust the way My Computer shows you files and folders on your disk drives. You can opt to see big icons, little icons, filename lists — oh, the list just goes on and on. The following information details your options for looking at the information in My Computer.

Toolbar: All the windows in My Computer can include a toolbar. If you don't see the My Computer toolbar when you open the window, follow these steps:

1. Choose View.

2. Choose Toolbar.

3. Choose Standard buttons. Miraculously, the toolbar appears!

Address bar: Besides viewing the Standard buttons, you can also choose to view the Address bar. Follow these steps to bring the Address bar into view:

1. Choose View.

2. Choose Toolbar.

3. Choose Address Bar.

The Address bar is *everywhere*. Any folder you open has the Address bar. Click the down arrow and double-click any of the folders or icons to open a folder.

Links bar: The Links bar enables you to link directly to different parts of the Internet. Microsoft sort of shoves the Internet down your throat this way. Follow these steps to view the Links bar:

1. Choose View.

2. Choose Toolbar.

3. Choose Links.

You have to stretch the My Computer dialog box to see all these links. You do this by putting your cursor on either the left or right edge of the box until the cursor turns into a double-headed arrow. Click and drag the edge of the box as far left or right as you can. Then drag the opposite edge.

Status bar: Windows in My Computer also use a status bar. This is a strip along the bottom of the window used by most programs to display extra information or options.

The status bar in My Computer tells you how many files or folders are selected and their total size. If no files or folders are selected, the status bar tells you how many files and folders are in the current window and their total size. If you select one file or folder, the total size of that one file is displayed on the status bar.

Follow these steps to see the status bar:

1. Double-click My Computer.

2. Choose <u>V</u>iew.

3. Choose Status <u>B</u>ar.

Follow these same steps to remove the status bar so that you can see more of your stuff in the window. By choosing the Status <u>B</u>ar option a second time, you turn off its display.

Large icon view: The most popular way to view information in My Computer is with large icons. This is the way that My Computer initially shows you information, which I think can be quite handy because the icons are easy to read.

Follow these steps if your computer isn't already set up to display large icons:

1. Double-click My Computer.

2. Choose <u>V</u>iew.

3. Choose Lar<u>g</u>e Icons.

Small icon view: Small icon view is handy when a folder contains many files and you want to see more than one in a window. Choose the view that works best for you.

Follow these steps to see small icons:

1. Double-click My Computer.

2. Choose <u>V</u>iew.

3. Choose S<u>m</u>all Icons.

In either view, Large Icons or Small Icons, you can move the icons around in the window, arranging them as you please. Just drag an icon to a new spot in the window and it stays there. This isn't possible with the List view, however, which always shows smaller icons in neat columns.

Details view: The Details view of My Computer is for those true fans of DOS or the real computer nerds out there. Details view displays the files by icon, name, size in bytes, type of file, and, finally, the date on which it was created or last modified, in neat little columns.

Follow these step to use Details view:

1. Double-click My Computer.

2. Choose View.

3. Choose Details.

Sorting items in My Computer: You can sort the items in a window in a number of ways:

✔ By Drive Letter

✔ By Type

✔ By Size

✔ By Free Space

Follow these steps to sort your information:

1. Double-click My Computer.

2. Choose View.

3. Choose Arrange Icons. A submenu appears from which you can choose how to sort the icons in the window.

If you like things in order, follow these steps:

1. Double-click My Computer.

2. Choose View.

3. Choose Arrange Icons.

4. Choose Auto Arrange. This automatically places icons in neat rows and columns.

My Documents Folder

The My Documents folder is your special folder in Windows. It's the place in which your documents are usually saved by default in Windows unless you specify another folder. Many of the applications that are part of Windows, as well as other programs you may use, attempt to save files first in the My Documents folder.

If you're using Windows 95, you may or may not have a My Documents folder. (You have it if you installed Microsoft Office 95 or later.) If you don't have a My Documents folder, you can create it. *See also* "Creating a Folder" earlier in this part.

All your new documents should be created in the My Documents folder or a subfolder you create in My Documents. This keeps all your work in one general area.

The Root Folder

Every disk has at least one main folder, called the *root* folder. Similar to a tree, all other folders on the disk branch out from the root folder. So the root folder is simply the main folder on the disk drive.

When you click a disk drive icon in My Computer or Explorer, the files and folders you see are all stored in the root folder.

The root folder is also called the *root directory.*

Working with Files

Windows stores information in files. Whether it's a word processing document, a picture, an e-mail message, or just a doodle, it's stored in a file on a disk. The Save command puts the file there. The Open command opens the file for editing. Windows gives you various tools to keep these files organized. You have the Copy, Cut, and Paste commands for moving and removing files, the Rename command for, obviously, renaming a file, and the Find command for finding files that you've misplaced.

In this part . . .

Finding Files and Programs

To find a file in Windows, you use the Find command. To successfully find a file, you need to know something about it. Knowing one or more of the following tidbits can help you quickly find any file on your computer:

- ✔ The file's name, or at least part of it

- ✔ Any text in the file — words or parts of sentences that you may remember

- ✔ The date the file was created, last saved to disk, or modified

- ✔ The file's type

- ✔ The program that created the file

- ✔ The size of the file

If you have to use the Find command, it's often a sign that the files (or folders) weren't organized or named well. The trick to keeping yourself sane is good organization and naming your files and folders logically. *See also* Part V to find out more about organizing your folders.

Follow these steps to find a file:

1. Click the Start button.

2. Choose Find.

3. Choose Files or Folders.

4. Describe the lost file by filling in as much information about it as you can:

- • If you know the file's name, type the full filename in the Named text box.

- If you don't know the entire name, use asterisks (*) to replace the part that you don't know. For example, if you know the file contained the word *report,* you can type ***report*** in the Named box. If you know that the file started with the letters NU, you can type **NU*** in the Named box.

5. Choose the proper drive — either hard drive or floppy drive. If you're not sure which hard drive the file is on, choose the Local hard drives option (if that option is available). Otherwise, drive C is generally your best choice.

6. Put a check mark by Include subfolders (if it's not already checked).

7. Click the Find Now button, which sends Windows off on a merry chase to locate the file you requested. One of two things happens when it's finished:

   - **The file isn't found.** You see the text There are no items to show in this view displayed, along with the dismal counter (in the lower-left part of the dialog box) that says 0 file(s) found. Oh well. Try again.

   - **The file is found.** Any files matching your specifications are displayed in the (new) bottom part of the Find dialog box.

8. Do something with the file. Double-clicking the file opens it.

9. Close the Find dialog box by clicking the Close (X) box in the upper-right corner.

Managing Files

You manage and organize files primarily in My Computer or Windows Explorer. I prefer using Explorer to work with files because the files are listed in such a neat and organized fashion.

Selecting files

To select a single file, locate its icon in My Computer or Explorer. Click that icon once with the mouse. This step selects the file, which appears highlighted on-screen. The file is now ready for action.

If you want to select a group of files, you have a few options:

✔ **Option 1:** Press and hold down the Ctrl key on your keyboard. Click all the files that you want selected as a group, one after the other. This method is known as *Control+clicking* files.

✔ **Option 2:** Lasso the files. This is especially easy to do when the files appear together in Icon view. Follow these steps to lasso the files:

1. Start in the upper-left corner above the file group that you want to select; click and hold down the mouse button.

2. Drag down and to the right to create a rectangle surrounding the file icons that you want to select.

3. Release the mouse button. All the files you lassoed are selected as a group.

✔ **Option 3:** To select *all* the files in a folder, choose Edit⇨ Select All. To deselect a file from a group, just press Ctrl while you click the file.

✔ **Option 4:** To select contiguous files, press the Shift key and click the first and last file. This selects all the files in between.

The keyboard shortcut for selecting all the files in a folder is Ctrl+A.

Moving files

Follow these steps to cut and paste (move) a file:

1. Use My Computer or Explorer to locate the file(s) that you want to move.

2. Click the file once to select it.

3. Choose Edit from the menu bar.

4. Choose Cut.

5. Open the folder where you want to paste (move) the file. Again, use the Explorer or My Computer program to hunt down the proper destination folder. You can also click the Cut button on the toolbar or use the keyboard shortcut Ctrl+X.

6. Choose Edit.

7. Choose Paste. To paste a file (or text or a graphic), you can also click the Paste button on the toolbar or use the keyboard shortcut Ctrl+V.

Copying a file

Copying and pasting a file works just like cutting and pasting, but the file is copied instead of moved. The original file remains where it was, fully intact. So after copying, you have two copies of the same file (or group of files if you're copying a bunch of them).

Follow these steps to copy and paste a file:

1. Use My Computer or Explorer to locate the file(s) that you want to copy.

2. Click the file once to select it.

3. Choose Edit.

4. Choose Copy. You can also use the Copy button on the toolbar (if visible) or click the keyboard shortcut Ctrl+C.

5. Use the Explorer or My Computer program to hunt down and open the proper destination folder where you want the file pasted (copied to).

6. Choose Edit.

7. Choose Paste. You can also use the Paste button on the toolbar or click the keyboard shortcut Ctrl+V.

Remember: When you paste the file, you're pasting a full copy. The original file remains untouched.

Deleting files

You are allowed to delete old, useless files. Really, it's okay. Old files just take up space and get in the way.

Follow these steps to delete a file:

1. Use My Computer or Explorer to find the file that you want to delete.

2. Click once to select the file.

3. Choose File from the menu bar.

4. Choose Delete. This moves the file over to the Recycle Bin (which is the trash bin for all the deleted files and folders). From there, you can undelete the file if you later decide you want it — and you haven't emptied the Recycle Bin.

Here a few other ways to delete a selected file:

✔ Press the Delete key on the keyboard.

✔ Click the Delete button on the toolbar (if the toolbar is visible on-screen).

✔ Use the mouse to click and drag the file into the Recycle Bin icon on the desktop.

Never delete any file in the Windows folder or any of the folders in the Windows folder. Never delete any file in the root folder of a hard drive. To be safe, never delete any file unless you created it yourself.

Undeleting files

Sometimes, you may change your mind about your deleted file and want it back. Follow these steps to undelete a file:

1. Double-click the Recycle Bin icon located on the desktop.

2. Click once to select the file that you want to undelete.

3. Choose File from the menu bar.

4. Choose Restore. The file is removed from the Recycle Bin and moved back into the folder where it started.

5. Click the window's Close (X) button in the upper-right corner to close the Recycle Bin window.

You can restore files from the Recycle Bin for quite some time. Eventually, the Recycle Bin automatically starts deleting really old files, but you do have some waiting time before that happens. If you've really goofed and want to undelete a bunch of files, you can use the lasso method to select files, or you can use the Ctrl+click and Shift+click methods. **See also** Options 1 and 4 in the "Selecting Files" section earlier in this part.

To display files in the order (by date) in which they were deleted, choose View⇨Arrange Icons⇨by Delete Date. This makes it easy to find any recently departed files that you may want back.

Naming and Renaming Files

You have to name a file when you want to save it to a disk. Most programs work similarly in the way you save and name a file. In the following steps, I use the WordPad program, which comes with Windows. Feel free to open whatever program you like to use.

Follow these steps to name a file:

1. Click the Start button.

2. Choose Programs.

3. Choose Accessories.

4. Choose WordPad.

5. Type something clever that you want to save.

6. Choose File from the menu bar.

7. Choose Save As. The Save As dialog box appears, and a default name appears in the File Name text box. You can use the default name or type a new one. You can also click the arrow in the Save In box if you want to store the file somewhere besides the default folder displayed there.

8. Click the Save button to save the file.

The following list offers some suggestions for things that you should consider when you name a file:

✔ **Be brief:** The best filenames are brief yet descriptive, like the following examples:

- Stocks

- Outline

- Chapter 1

- Itinerary

If you give a file a name that's too long, you may make a typing error when you try to retrieve it; then Windows won't be able to open the file. In addition, the rows of files listed in the Open and Save dialog boxes get farther and farther apart if a long file-name is in the list.

✔ **Use only letters, numbers, and spaces:** Filenames can contain just about any key that you can press on the keyboard. Even so, it's best to stick with letters, numbers, and spaces. Whether you use uppercase and lowercase for your filenames doesn't matter to Microsoft Windows. *See also* the following section, "Don't name a file this way!," for more information about filenames.

✔ **Be descriptive:** The filename should be illustrative of what's in the file.

Don't name a file this way!

Windows gets mad if you use any of these characters to name a file:

* / : < > ? \ |

Each of these characters holds a special meaning to Windows (or DOS). Nothing bad happens if you attempt to use these characters — Windows just refuses to save the file or asks you to change the filename. And although you can use any number of periods in a filename, you cannot name a file with all periods.

The filename extension

The last part of a filename is typically a period followed by one to three characters. This last part is called the *filename extension*. It is used by Windows to identify the file's type. For example, a *.bmp* ending to a filename indicates that the file is a Paint graphics image; *.doc* indicates a document created by WordPad or Microsoft Word.

You never have to type these extensions when you name or rename a file. In fact, you shouldn't. Windows automatically adds the extensions for you as you give the file a name and save it.

Renaming a file

Sometimes, you may give a file a name that is anything but descriptive. Don't worry — just rename the file.

Follow these steps to rename a file:

1. Use Windows Explorer to locate a file that you want to rename. *See also* "Finding Files and Programs" at the beginning of this part for more information about finding files on disk.

2. Select the file by clicking it once.

3. Choose File.

4. Choose Rename from the list of options.

5. Type a new name.

6. Press the Enter key to lock in the new name.

All files *must* have a name. If you don't give the file a name (if you try to leave it blank), Windows warns you that you must name your file.

You can also rename a file by right-clicking it and choosing Rename from the shortcut menu. Or you can click the file's icon once and choose File⇨Rename from the menu.

Using the Open Dialog Box

The Open dialog box is a tool used to open files and folders. If you want to work on a document that you previously saved, you use the Open dialog box. The following figure illustrates a typical Open dialog box.

Follow these steps to use the Open dialog box to open a file:

1. Choose File.

2. Choose Open. The Open dialog box appears.

3. If you find your file, double-click to open it. If you can't find your file, look in another folder. If nothing interests you in that folder, click the Up button (the button displaying a file folder with an upward-pointing arrow) at the top of the Open dialog box to go back up one level in the file structure. Continue opening folders to find the one you want.

   If you still can't find your file, switch disk drives. All the disk drives are listed in the Open dialog box in the Look In area. Click the down arrow to see more disk drives listed (if you have them, which you may not).

4. When you find your file, click Open.

Using the Save As Dialog Box

The Save As dialog box is an important dialog box in Windows. It's the key to organizing your files in a logical manner.

You use the Save As dialog box when you create something — a document, a spreadsheet, a picture, whatever — and you're ready to save your creation. In the Save As dialog box, you decide where you are going to "file" your document and what you are going to name it.

Follow these steps to use the Save As dialog box:

1. Choose File from the menu bar.

2. Choose Save As.

Save As		? X
Save in: My Documents		
Audio	My Pictures	Video
Boring New Folder	New Folder	Work
Font Stowage	Personal	07
Graphics	Raw Text Files	Airline food
Great American Novel	Temporary	Airport 200
HTML files	Theater	All My Font
File name: Document		Save
Save as type: Word for Windows 6.0		Cancel

3. Check the Save in drop-down list to see which folder the Save As dialog box wants to put your document in. In the preceding figure, it says My Documents. That's where your document will be saved. If that isn't what you want, move on to the next step. If the My Documents folder is okay, skip to Step 6 to give the file a descriptive name.

4. Hunt for the folder in which you want to save your file. The best way to find a folder is to start at the root. To get to the root folder, you must choose a hard drive from the Save in drop-down list (at the top of the dialog box).

5. Locate the folder — or the folder that contains the folder (sub-folder) — in which you want to save your information and open it. For example, open your Work folder or the My Documents folder. When you find the folder you want, move on to Step 6.

6. Type a name for the saved file in the File name text box. **See also** "Naming and Renaming Files" earlier in this part.

7. Click the Save button.

After you save your stuff once, you can use the File➪Save command to resave your file to disk periodically.

In Windows 98 and Windows 2000, the Save As dialog box initially puts your document in the My Documents folder. That's fine, unless your PC doesn't have a My Documents folder or some other folder is used instead.

Here are a few more tips for saving files:

✔ Avoid the temptation to save your file in the root folder. This isn't a good organizational tactic, and your root folder eventually gets out of control with tons of files. It would be like putting all your files in one big box.

✔ Remember that you can also click the Create New Folder button in the Save As dialog box to create a new folder. Name the folder and then open it to save your work right then and there.

✔ If you want to save your file to disk in another spot, give it a new name, or save it as another type of file, you need to use the Save As dialog box again. In that case, choose File⊃Save As from the menu.

In many applications, you can use the keyboard shortcut for saving a file, Ctrl+S, or you can click the Save button found on the toolbar.

Printing Your Work

Your computer needs a monitor and keyboard. You probably already figured this out. But another important toy that you need is the printer. A printer is a device that produces an image on paper and provides the proof that, yes, you do actually work.

The image that a printer produces can be text or graphics, and it can be printed in black ink or in full color. Using a printer is often your last step in creating something on the PC, so you want that final image to be as good as possible.

Printers are judged by the quality of the images they produce and by their price. Generally, you can pay anywhere from just over $100 to thousands of dollars for a printer.

In this part...

Checking Out Your Printer's Control Panel

Every printer has a control panel. More expensive models have LCD screens that display information relating to your printer. Less expensive printers may just have an on/off button and a page eject button.

Locate your printer's control panel now and find these two buttons:

✔ **The on-line or select button:** This tells your printer whether or not to print. When the printer is off-line or deselected, the computer can't print. You may occasionally have to take the printer off-line to un-jam it because of a paper misfeed.

✔ **The form-feed button:** This button is used to eject a page of paper from the printer. *Remember:* Only when the printer is on-line or selected can the computer print.

Some laser printers may have an online button but no form-feed button. In that case, you need to refer to your printer's manual for information on doing a form-feed.

General Printing Tips

Printing is generally easy and can make your work look fabulous. The following tips can help make printing as painless as possible:

✔ **Ink:** Ink is obviously an important part of printing, so keep these points in mind:

- Keep a spare printer cartridge on hand — you don't want to be in the middle of printing a big report when you find that you're out of ink with no extras available.

- Never let your printer toner get low, and don't let ink cartridges go dry. You may think it saves money to squeeze out every last drop of ink, but it's not good for the printer.

- Many laser printers have a "toner low" light or warning message. When you first see it, you can take the toner out of the printer and rock it from side to side. This redistributes the toner and gets more mileage from it — but you can do this only once! Replace the old toner as soon as you see the "toner low" light again.

- Inkjet printers generally warn you that the ink cartridge is low, either on the printer's panel or on your computer's screen. Change the ink cartridge at once! Some printers are really stubborn about this and will continually annoy you with warnings about low ink until you change the cartridge.

✔ **Location:** Place your printer somewhere close — preferably within arm's reach of your PC. You may find that you like to frequently print a single page as you work, and you want to be close enough to easily grab the page from the printer.

✔ **Paper:** You can't print without paper, so remember the following points:

- Printers don't come with paper — you have to buy it separately. Be sure to buy the proper paper for your printer.

- Stock up on paper — you'll be glad you did when you're printing large amounts of stuff. Go to one of those discount paper warehouse places and buy a few boxes to keep on hand.

- Keep all your paper and envelope supplies near your printer for easy access.

- If you see an arrow on one side of the outside paper wrapping, it usually indicates whether the top side is up or down.

✔ **Plugging in:** You have to properly connect everything before you print:

- If your PC has more than one printer port, plug your printer into LPT1, which is the first printer port.

- Printers don't come with cables! You must buy the cable separately from the printer.

- The printer cable can be no more than 20 feet long. After 20 feet, the transfer of information isn't always reliable. You probably won't have to worry about cable length because the best place for your printer is within arm's reach.

✔ **Print Preview:** It's a good idea to preview your work before you start printing so that you're sure to print exactly what you want to print. Many Windows programs have a File➪Print Preview command that lets you review the page before it's printed.

✔ **Print toolbar icon:** Many applications sport a Print toolbar icon. If that's the case in the application you're using, you can click that button to quickly print your document. Be forewarned though: Clicking the Print toolbar icon will use the last printer you chose to use, provided you have more than one printer you can use.

✔ **Saving:** Always save your stuff before you print — it's a good habit to get into. That way, if you run into any problems during printing that causes you to have to reboot, all your hard work is safe.

✔ **Second printer:** Your computer is capable of handling two printers! However, your PC needs a second printer port to handle both printers.

✔ **Sideways printing:** Some programs may not use the Paper tab in the printer's Properties dialog box for selecting the paper size and orientation (the direction that you want your text or image to print on the page). In Microsoft Word, for example, you choose File⇨Page Setup and then choose the Paper Size tab. **See also** "Printing sideways" later in this part.

Getting Your Printer Set Up

Follow these steps to set up your printer:

1. Turn your computer off. Make sure that the printer is off as well.

2. Plug one end of the printer cable into the printer port on the back of your PC's console. You find a connection called the printer port on the rear of the PC's console. It may be labeled as LPT1.

3. Plug the other end of the cable into the printer.

4. Plug the printer's power cord into the wall socket. Do not plug the printer into an Uninterruptible Power Supply (UPS) — printers should be plugged directly into the wall, not into a power strip or UPS. **See also** Part XIV for more information about the UPS.

That completes the installation of your physical printer (also known as the hardware installation). The "Printer Software" section later in this part tells you how to install the software you need to run your printer.

Adding paper

Paper is a necessity when you use a printer. Otherwise, what's the point? Both inkjet and laser printers use sheets of paper, similar to photocopier paper. That continuous fan-fold paper that you may have seen is for older impact (dot-matrix) printers that you'll probably never use.

For inkjet printers, load the paper into the tray — either near the printer's bottom or sticking out the top, depending on how your printer's paper tray works.

Some laser printers require that you fill a cartridge with paper, similar to the way a copy machine works. Slide the cartridge all the way into the printer after it's loaded.

Some printers are capable of handling larger-sized paper, such as legal or tabloid. If yours can use these sizes, make sure that you load the paper properly and tell Windows or your software application that you're using a different size of paper.

Check your printer to see how the paper goes in — either face down or face up — and note which side is the top. You need to know this when you print envelopes or checks (you can print checks if you use personal finance software), or if you want to print something on the reverse side of a page that has already been printed.

Don't use erasable bond and other fancy "dusted" papers in your laser printer. Those papers have talcum powder coatings that come off in your laser printer and gum up the printing device on your printer.

Adding ink

You are responsible for loading your printer with ink and changing it when it's empty. Just like you keep gas in your car, you must keep ink in your printer. Different kinds of printers use different kinds of cartridges, as the following list explains:

✔ **Inkjet printers:** These printers use ink cartridges. Carefully unwrap the foil around the new cartridge and remove any tape or covering, according to package instructions. Then insert the ink cartridge into the printer, again following the instructions for your specific printer.

✔ **Laser printers:** These printers require drop-in toner cartridges. They are easy to install and come with their own instructions. Some manufacturers sell their cartridges with return envelopes so that you can send the old cartridge back to the factory for recycling or proper disposal.

You can take your old toner cartridge and get it "recharged." You can take it to a special place that cleans the old cartridge and refills it with toner. This actually works and is often cheaper than buying a whole new cartridge. Ask the people at your local computer store for the nearest place to get your cartridge recharged.

Inkjet Printers

Two major types of printers that are popular today are the inkjet printer and the laser printer.

Inkjet printers are the most popular type of computer printer sold today. They're primarily color printers, and they produce high-quality text or graphics on just about any type of paper. Some higher-end inkjet printers are even capable of photographic quality output.

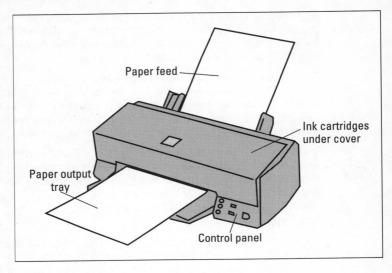

This figure illustrates a typical inkjet printer. These printers work by literally lobbing tiny balls of ink onto paper. These tiny ink balls stick to the paper, so this type of printer needs no ribbon or toner cartridge. The ink sprays directly onto the paper from multiple tiny jets: thus, the name inkjet.

Most inkjet printers print with both color and black inks. The ink is stored in tiny cartridges. Typically, one cartridge contains black ink and another contains the colored inks.

Inkjet printers can be fairly inexpensive. Some of the low-end models can be purchased for only a couple hundred dollars, and you may find that their quality and speed is fine for your needs. Higher-end models produce a better image, faster, but they can cost from $800 to over $1,000. However, the broad price range of the inkjet printer makes it one of the best-suited printers for any PC.

Price shouldn't necessarily be the only factor when picking a printer. Quality of the printing should be a major reason for picking a printer. Visit one of the big mega computer stores where you can see the quality of every printer the store is selling. This makes choosing a printer much easier, and you also won't be surprised by the quality of the printing.

Buying ink cartridges

With an inkjet printer, you get an inexpensive computer printer that prints very well (and prints in color!). The price you pay for this quality is that inkjet ink cartridges cost a ton! In fact, if you do a lot of printing, you may spend twice as much a year on ink cartridges as you did on the actual printer. If possible, try to buy inkjet cartridges in bulk. Several online and mail-order dealers offer cheap prices on ink cartridges that typically are better than what you can find in an office supply store or other local retailer.

Be sure to keep the catalog number of your ink cartridge so that you can easily reorder the proper cartridge. And don't be lured into buying off-brand cartridges. If the ink formula isn't just right, problems can occur (such as burnt out or clogged print heads). You should generally buy the name brand ink for your printer.

Remember: You don't always have to print in color with an inkjet printer! You can also just print in black ink, which saves the pricey color cartridge from running low.

Buying special paper

Your inkjet printer can print on just about any type of paper. However, more expensive paper produces a better image.

My favorite type of inkjet paper is actually called laser paper. It has a polished look to it and a subtle waxy feel. Colors look better on this paper, and black ink text documents have a much nicer feel than printing on regular photocopier paper.

The best, and the most outrageously expensive, paper to buy is special photographic paper. Using this paper with your printer's high-quality mode results in a color image that looks very close to a photograph. But at $1 per sheet (this price can vary), this kind of paper is best used for special occasions.

Here's another fun paper to use: iron-on transfer paper. You can print an image (you have to print it in reverse) and then use an iron to "weld" that image to a T-shirt.

Laser Printers

Laser printers are for heavy workloads and are primarily used in the office. Laser printers are great for producing both text and graphics, but usually only in black and white. Color laser printers are available, but they're outrageously expensive — especially when a low-cost inkjet printer can do most color jobs.

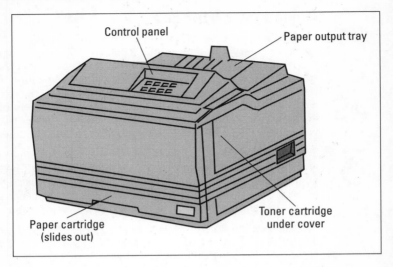

Control panel

Paper output tray

Paper cartridge
(slides out)

Toner cartridge
under cover

As you can see in this figure, a laser printer often resembles a squat copy machine. Generally, you place the paper into a tray, which then slides into the printer. The paper scrolls through the printer, and the final result slides out on top.

Laser printers are generally more expensive than inkjet printers — and a bit faster. Color laser printers are quite expensive, but their color quality is usually better than inkjets.

 Beware of a laser printer's speed rating. The speed is measured in pages per minute (ppm), and it can be deceptive. Laser printers print faster when they print the same image over and over, which is how they are measured for the ppm rating. Actual output under normal circumstances is slower.

Printer Software

One of the first questions that Microsoft Windows asks you during set up is "Which printer are you using?" I'm sure that you, or whoever set up your computer, followed the steps and chose the proper printer. If that's your situation, you don't have to work through the steps in this section.

If you didn't have a printer to choose at the time, however, and are just now adding one, you need to install the printer software, called a *driver*. The printer driver is the software that controls a printer. **See also** Part XI to find out more about drivers.

Follow these steps to install the printer software:

1. Connect your printer to the PC.

2. Turn your printer on and load it with paper.

3. Click the Start button.

4. Choose Settings.

5. Choose Printers. A window appears listing all the printers that you may already have connected to your PC, including network printers. There is also a special Add Printer icon.

6. Double-click the Add Printer icon. The Add Printer Wizard appears, and the remaining steps in this list guide you through using this Wizard.

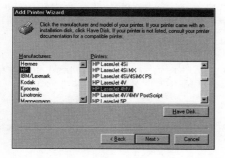

7. Click the Next button.

8. If you're not setting up a network printer, click the Next button. If you are setting up a network printer, have someone help you at this point.

9. From the list provided in the dialog box, select your printer's manufacturer and then select the appropriate model number. If your printer isn't listed, you have to use the special installation disk that should have been packaged with the printer. If this is your situation, insert the disk into your floppy drive, click the Have Disk button, and browse to the floppy drive containing the disk.

10. Click the Next button.

11. Pick the printer port from the list. The printer port is probably LPT1, your first printer port.

12. Click the Next button.

13. Click the Next button again.

14. Click Finish.

Hey, you did it! You're finished.

You can now print a test page on your printer to ensure that your printer is connected properly and that everything is working as it should.

Working with Your Printer

All you need to do to get your printer to work (after everything is hooked up and the software is installed) is to flip the switch on.

Most printers can be left on all the time. But you may want to turn off your laser printer because it uses a lot of energy. However, Energy Star laser printers can be left on all the time because these printers run in a low-power mode when they're not working.

You can leave an inkjet printer on all the time because they don't use much energy, or you can turn it off when you finish printing.

Printing something

All applications support the same print command, so the following steps work the same, regardless of the program you use.

Follow these steps to print:

1. Choose File from the menu bar.

2. Choose Print.

3. Select the printer next to Name: if you have more than one printer to choose from (which would be the case if you had a separate color printer or if you were on a network).

4. Choose the pages you want to print. Sometimes you may want to print only page 3 instead of the whole document.

5. Choose the number of copies you want to print. Click the Collate button if you want the pages printed in order. For example, if you want 5 copies of a 10-page document, choosing Collate tells the printer to sort the copies. You get pages 1 through 10 sequentially 5 times rather than 10 pages of page 1, 10 pages of page 2, and so on.

6. Click OK in the Print dialog box.

The keyboard shortcut for the print command is Ctrl+P.

Printing sideways

Printing on a sheet of paper long-ways is called printing in landscape mode. Printing in landscape mode looks like you're printing your work sideways. Your text goes from left to right — long-ways on the page. This is especially good for information that requires lots of columns, such as in a spreadsheet.

Follow these steps to use landscape mode and print sideways:

1. Choose File from the menu bar.

2. Choose Print from the list of options. The Print dialog box opens.

3. Click the Properties button.

4. Click the Paper tab to bring that panel forward.

5. Click the Landscape option.

6. Click OK to close the Paper tab and return to the Print dialog box.

7. Click OK to print in landscape mode.

Printing the screen

Printing the screen means printing a copy of exactly what is on your screen. This capability can come in handy when you need a hard copy of your screen to refer to when, for example, you're writing a book about your personal computer and you need an example of something on your computer screen — just like you've seen in this book.

Follow these steps to print a copy of your Windows desktop or some window on the screen:

1. Arrange the screen so that it looks the way that you want to see it printed.

2. If you want a snapshot of the whole screen, press the Print Scrn key on your keyboard. If you want a snapshot of only the top window on the screen, press Alt+Print Scrn. The image of the screen is now stored on the Windows Clipboard.

3. Click the Start button.

4. Choose Programs.

5. Choose Accessories.

6. Choose Paint. The Paint program opens.

7. Choose Edit from the Paint menu bar.

8. Choose Paste. This takes the screen image you just placed on the Clipboard and pastes it into the Paint program. If a warning box tells you that the image is too big, click Yes. This is telling the Paint program that yes, you would like the bitmap enlarged.

9. Choose File from the Paint menu bar.

10. Choose Print.

11. Click OK. The image from your screen prints to your printer.

Feeding an envelope

To stick an envelope into your printer, find the special envelope slot or open the front hatch of the printer. Generally, a special illustration on the hatch tells you which way to place the envelope: face up or down, and top-right or top-left. Then you work through the printing steps to tell your software to print the envelope.

Feeding an envelope to a printer is different for each type of printer, and each program has a different command for printing envelopes. Typically, you tell the program how the envelope goes into your printer so that it knows in which direction to print the address. If all else fails, you may have to refer to the printer manual and software documentation to figure out exactly how to use your printer.

Some printers require you to press the On-line or Select button to print the envelope.

Software Guide

Software is power. You can punch all kinds of key combinations and press all kinds of buttons, but it's the software that makes things happen. Software entertains you, balances checkbooks, and makes you an artist. Maybe software is in the works now to provide world peace.

In this part . . .

Buying Software

Buying software is part of the computer-buying process. You decide what software you want to run *first,* and then you choose the hardware that can run it.

If you're serious about making smart software investments (you can waste a lot of money on useless software), check out *Buying a Computer For Dummies* by Dan Gookin (published by IDG Books Worldwide, Inc.).

Here are some software-buying tips to help you make educated choices:

- ✔ See what other people are using. Are they happy with the software? Are they getting their tasks done?

- ✔ Make sure that you buy software that fits your needs, not just what's cheap and popular.

- ✔ Ask if you can try the software before you buy it.

- ✔ Have someone at the store demonstrate the software for you.

- ✔ Always check out a store's return policy on software.

- ✔ Check the software's requirements. They should match your computer's hardware inventory. You don't want to buy software for a Macintosh if you're running Microsoft Windows.

Installing Software

You automatically have some software on your new computer when you buy it. But it may not be enough for you. So head off to your local computer store, check out the rows and rows of software products, pick out what you want, bring it home, open the box, and then the fun begins — you get to install it!

Follow these steps to install software:

1. Find and read the information that says "Read Me First."

2. Put the Installation disk into your disk drive. If you have multiple disks in your software, find the disk marked with the words "Installation" or "Setup" or "Disk 1," and place that disk in the proper disk drive. If you're installing from floppy disks and the program has more than one floppy disk, these disks are numbered. Put them in a neat stack, in order, with Disk 1 on top. This way, you won't put the wrong disk in or lose track of which disk you were working on.

3. Start the Installation program.

   - The installation program may run automatically when you insert the CD into the CD-ROM drive. If this is the case, just read the instructions on the screen.

   - If the installation program doesn't start automatically, you need to run it yourself. Continue with these steps *only* if your CD doesn't install automatically.

4. Click the Start Button.

5. Choose Settings.

6. Choose Control Panel.

7. Double-click the Add/Remove Programs icon.

8. Click the Install/Uninstall tab to bring it forward, if it isn't already front and center.

9. Click the Install button.

10. Read the screen carefully and click the Next button as necessary. Read all following screens thoroughly. If your eyes glaze over when this information appears, you may miss some important information. If you are updating an older version of a program, the installation program may tell you that it is going to erase the older version, unless you tell it not to. You don't want to miss this kind of information. If you like the old version and don't want to get rid of it, you have to click Cancel so that the new software isn't installed. If you don't care, go ahead and click Continue.

11. Choose various options as you're prompted. The options depend on the software that you're installing.

12. Answer all questions as they appear on-screen. You may be asked your name and a company name or for a serial number. You can usually find the serial number inside the manual, on the CD-ROM case, on the first disk in the stack of 3½-inch disks, or on a separate card located with the rest of the information in the software box.

13. Choose any default options. When asked to make a decision, the option already selected (the default) is typically the best option. Only change from the default if you're sure that another option is a better choice. Eventually, the files start copying to your computer.

14. You may or may not be asked to restart your computer at this point. If you are asked to reset, you should go ahead and do it now so you don't forget to do it later. If the computer asks you to restart, it means that your software won't work until you do so.

Congratulations! You're ready to start using the program.

Granted, these are general steps. Your new software should come with more specific instructions. Each software package is a little different and requires different steps.

Remember: Read everything carefully. Don't forget to check for information on the back side of the cover sheet that shows through the CD case. Installation steps may be hidden there.

I tend to keep the information that comes in the software box. The quick reference card is sometimes more helpful than the manual. And you may need the card with the serial number on it. Some software companies won't let you upgrade if you don't have the serial number of your current version.

Software programs are fairly simple to install, especially games. If you can't find any of the Read Me files, look on the cover of the CD case where this information is usually stored. Also remember to register your software. This enables you to receive support programs that may not otherwise be available.

Software for Home and Office

If you ever visit one of those huge computer superstores, you're sure to find the enormous amount of software overwhelming. Wow! How do you choose what to get? Not to worry. I'm here to help.

Antivirus Software

Antivirus software is available mostly, in my opinion, to scare the general public. If you tend to scare easily, go ahead and look into the antivirus software. But if you really don't want to catch a computer virus, follow these preventive measures:

✔ Don't share floppy disks with other computer users.

✔ Don't open e-mail attachments from anyone you don't know.

You cannot get a virus through a plain text e-mail (in other words, just the messages). You cannot get a virus through the phone lines by using your modem. ***See also*** Part XII to find out more on how to avoid getting a computer virus.

If you are in a business in which sharing disks is a necessity, a few programs out there work well. Norton AntiVirus and McAfee VirusScan are two that I recommend.

Database

Database programs are designed to organize, sort, and report any type of information (otherwise known as *data,* which is pronounced *day-tuh*).

Database programs come in three flavors:

- **Free-form database:** This type works best when you're organizing a big file that's full of random information. For example, if you search for the word *tomato,* the database retrieves every paragraph mentioning *tomato,* which may bring up a grocery list or a favorite recipe.

- **Flat file database:** This database retrieves information that's been organized into fields, records, and files so that you can request information about people named Dan who drive Hummers and vote Libertarian. This database requires the information to be organized in specific ways.

- **Relational database:** This is the most powerful type of database. The data is organized in tables that are "related" by a common field or column.

Some database programs have all the forms ready and you need only fill in the blanks. Other databases require you to make the forms and design how everything looks. More complex databases make you do *everything,* which includes writing the program that runs the database.

Most people don't need a database, although they are handy in organizing information, such as client lists.

The mailing list database is a good example of one type of database that just about anyone can use. This database is designed to contain names, addresses, phone numbers, and other information about people. Its primary purpose is to allow you to print out a list for special occasions — such as address labels for dinner party invitations.

Before you go hunting for a database, see if your computer has Microsoft Works. It contains a pretty decent database that should fit most needs.

Desktop publishing

You use a word processor for composing text. You use a graphics program to create graphics. Then you use a desktop publishing program that takes the text and graphics and merges them for an excellent-looking document. However, desktop publishing software is expensive. Cheaper, "home" versions are available, but expect to pay quite a bit for the programs that the professionals use.

Microsoft Publisher is often installed on many computers. It can be found by clicking Start⇨Programs⇨Microsoft Publisher. The many Wizards in Microsoft Publisher make using this program really easy. There's not a lot of room for being truly creative, like Adobe PageMaker or QuarkXPress provides. But these last two are more difficult to use.

Education

Educational software programs are not just for kids. Lots of fun software is available to teach the basics of identifying shapes or learning ABCs, but you can also find educational software that can teach you a new language, how to type, how to read music, or help you learn human anatomy.

Educational software comes in different types. Mavis Beacon (oh, Mavis!) teaches typing through a series of drills cleverly disguised as games. Dr. Seuss's ABCs is a read-along computer "book" that educates as it entertains. Encarta is great encyclopedia software with samples of classical music and African poetry. My least favorite type, however, is the book-on-the-screen software. No one wants to sit there and read text on a computer screen. It's just not fun.

The best way to find respectable educational software is to ask people who already use the software (your friends, family, and coworkers). You can also check family and computer magazines for reviews of the software. Make sure that you find a real review and not just a book report of what the software does. The review should have both good and possibly bad things about the software.

You should heed these educational software warnings:

- ✔ **Read the purpose of the software first:** Avoid game software that pretends to be educational. This happens often in software designed for young children. The software can have several games, puzzles, and painting, but it lacks educational information.

- ✔ **Make sure that the software is compatible with your computer:** Read the side of the software box to make sure that your operating system is listed. (For example, find the text that says "This software works on Windows 95 and Windows 98.")

- ✔ **Avoid software that lists its best feature as "hand-eye coordination":** Working with a mouse, playing catch, or hitting a ball with a bat are the best hand-eye coordination exercises available.

✔ **Read the software box for any additional equipment that is needed:** For example, does the software require a joystick or a special sound card?

✔ **Don't confuse educational software with reference software:** Microsoft's Encarta encyclopedia is a great reference tool with lots of great information, but no educational activity is involved.

Games

Don't fool yourself. Games are time wasters. In fact, you should limit the amount of time children spend playing computer games. On the other hand, there are some fun games out there, so if you are installing games on your computer, do it right!

To play a game on your PC in the best possible way, your computer should be equipped with the following items:

✔ A Pentium II with MMX (or a Pentium III).

✔ A large hard drive.

✔ A CD-ROM drive. Nearly every game comes on a CD.

✔ A powerful graphics card. 3-D graphics is the best type of graphics card to get. More memory on the graphics card (up to 4MB) is even better.

✔ A sound card.

✔ A joystick, although this isn't always necessary because many games are playable using some combination of the mouse and the keyboard. If you do get a joystick, ensure that it's fully compatible with the game. Many of the flight-simulator games are geared to work best with a specific brand of joystick. If you know what brand you need before you buy a joystick, you'll get the best possible configuration.

Games use a ton of disk space. The more games you install, the more storage you can expect to dwindle away.

I recommend using drive D for games, if your PC has a drive D. Most people don't use drive D, which makes all its storage space up for grabs. Drive D in this case does not mean your CD-ROM drive. It means a second hard drive, where Drive C is your first hard drive.

Several categories of games are available:

- ✔ **Arcade:** These are the classic games — the kind where you shoot something, work puzzles, or maneuver through a maze.

- ✔ **Simulation:** The flight-simulator games tend to be the most popular. Other types of simulators include golf, war, battle simulations, sporting games, and the popular SimCity-like simulations in which you create and manage an artificial world.

- ✔ **Virtual reality:** Virtual reality games are where *you* become the person on the computer. You control yourself as you walk through a new world, see your enemies coming after you, and experience all the good and scary stuff. Games like Doom, Duke Nukem, Descent, Quake, Half-Life, Myst, and a host of Star Wars games are popular. But be warned: These games can get violent!

Games can be fun. Games can also be horrendously violent and inappropriate for kids, even though the packaging can draw them in. Two rating systems warn parents, or any PC game buyer, about the violent levels and adult contents of the games on the market.

The Entertainment Software Rating Board (ESRB) uses a five-level rating scale — similar to movie ratings — in evaluating games:

- ✔ **EC (Early childhood):** The game is designed for young children.

- ✔ **K-A (Kids to adult):** It's a G-rated game.

- ✔ **T (Teen):** The game has some violence and bad language, but nothing too offensive.

- ✔ **M (Mature audiences):** The game is intended for mature players only, preferably 17 years old or older.

- ✔ **AO (Adults only):** These games include strong sexual content or gross violence.

The Recreational Software Advisory Council (RSAC) is a voluntary rating decided by the software developer. The three categories are Violence, Nudity/Sex, and Language. For each category, a tiny thermometer rates the content at four levels, with level four being the most offensive.

You can get more information about these two rating systems from the following Web sites:

- ✔ **ESRB:** www.esrb.org/

- ✔ **RSAC:** www.rsac.org/

Personal finance

Personal finance software is designed to help with those tedious financial tasks that you must do, such as balance your checkbook, keep track of your receipts, and calculate interest on your savings account. Quicken seems to be the most popular accounting package today for both home and small businesses.

You can do all these tasks, and more, with Quicken:

- ✔ Write checks

- ✔ Categorize checks

- ✔ Print checks

- ✔ Reconcile your accounts

- ✔ Do a report on your spending habits

- ✔ Manage your portfolio

- ✔ Keep track of your stocks

- ✔ Check stock quotes online

- ✔ Schedule a loan and figure out how much money you can save by refinancing your home

- ✔ Keep track of your credit card expenses

- ✔ A whole bunch of other stuff that would make this list way too long

Spreadsheets

Think of a paper ledger book when you think of an electronic spreadsheet. Like an on-screen ledger, a spreadsheet provides you with a large grid of rows and columns (called "cells") for entering text, numbers, and formulas. The spreadsheet's job is to take the numbers and formulas that you enter, process the information, and perform the calculations.

The formula part is what makes the spreadsheet so powerful: You can add numbers in columns, compare values, and perform any number of odd or quirky mathematical operations or functions. The entire spreadsheet is instantly updated, too. You change one value, and all related information is also updated.

Spreadsheets, such as Microsoft Excel, are great for organizing any information that can fit into a grid — anything that requires columns or scheduling. And you can also use spreadsheets for doing graphics — spreadsheets make great pie charts!

Word processing

Word processing is all about writing, and that's why most people want to use the computer. Computers simplify the writing process and make it easier to produce professional-looking documents.

You can get three types of word-processing software:

- **Text editors:** A text editor is a word processor that does nothing but record the characters you type. They typically don't have margins, and they have little or no text formatting or few fonts. Text editors are fast and easy to use; they are great for keeping lists and jotting notes. Windows Notepad is an example of a text editor. It saves documents as plain text or ASCII files.

- **Word processors:** The word processor makes writing easy. You can edit, rewrite, spell-check, and format to make your text look professional. Word processors work with text just like text editors, but they add formatting, styles, proofing, and a bunch of features that make working fun, in addition to putting together a dynamite-looking document.

- **Desktop publishers:** Desktop publishing programs merge text and graphics into one document. *See also* "Desktop publishing" earlier in this part.

Uninstalling Software

To uninstall software, you run the Windows uninstall program. Each program that you install comes with its own uninstall feature. Typically, you can find the uninstall program if you click the Start button and choose Programs. Some programs that you installed previously may display a right-pointing arrow on the right side of the Programs menu. When you click that arrow, a submenu opens that often offers an Uninstall option.

If your software lacks an uninstall program, you can use the Windows Add/Remove Program feature.

Follow these steps to uninstall a program:

1. Click the Start button.

2. Choose Settings.

3. Click Control Panel.

4. Double-click the Add/Remove Program icon. Make sure that Install/Uninstall tab is forward. The list of programs available to uninstall is listed at the bottom of the dialog box.

5. Click the program that you want to uninstall. This selects the program for action.

6. Click the Add/Remove button. A Warning dialog box appears that asks you if you're sure you want to remove the selected program.

7. Click Yes.

For the best results, heed these uninstall warnings:

✔ *Never* try to uninstall *any* software by deleting it from your hard drive.

✔ *Never* delete any file that you did not create yourself. The file may be a key program in running some software you use all the time. (You can, however, delete any shortcuts that you create.)

You can also use the Add/Remove button to add individual components to your programs that, for some reason, don't always install when you are adding a new program, or that you had chosen not to install at the time.

Updating Software

You may notice that most software has a number after the name, such as Word 6.0. This is the update number so that you know which version — which update — of the software you have. Some computer users are obsessed with updating software. Is it necessary? You should order the update to your software only if it has features or makes modifications that you desperately need. Otherwise, if the current version is doing the job, don't bother.

Think carefully about each upgrade offer. Will you use the new features? Do you share files with someone who continually upgrades so that your lower version of the software is making it difficult to work together? After a while, newer versions of programs become incompatible with the older models. At that point, you may not have any choice but to upgrade.

Getting on the Internet

The Internet has evolved into more than just hooking up your telephone and computer. It's bigger than that. It's now a means by which you can talk to friends, shop, do homework, and find and listen to music. Because of the Internet, you don't even have to leave your house. Wow!

In this part . . .

ABCs of the Internet

The Internet comprises thousands and thousands of computers all over the world. Those computers send, receive, exchange, and store information. To dispel some rumors, the Internet is not a piece of software, and it's not a single computer owned by Bill Gates.

Before you can get at all the information on the Internet, you need the following five things:

- **Computer:** You can use any computer. Because the Internet comes through your PC's modem, it doesn't matter how fast your PC is.

- **Modem:** Get the fastest modem you can afford. There's nothing worse than waiting five minutes just to get connected to the Internet.

- **Internet software:** Windows comes with nearly all the software you need, but there are other Internet software packages available if you want to explore your options. The primary piece of Internet software you need is a Web browser, such as Internet Explorer or Netscape Communicator.

- **Money:** It costs money to access the Internet; think of it in the same way that you pay to get cable TV. Expect to pay anywhere from $5 to over $100 a month to get on the Internet, depending on the type of service you get. The average cost is about $20 a month.

- **An Internet Service Provider (ISP):** This is the only item you probably don't have. As an alternative to an ISP, you can use a national online service, such as America Online (AOL). Online services offer features that may make it a bit more user-friendly than a regular ISP, especially for folks new to the Internet.

Although the Internet isn't a program, you need special software to access the Internet and to send or retrieve information.

Before you look into getting on the Internet, check to see if you already have it. What? Yes. If you work for a large company, they may already provide Internet access through the network at your office. Ditto for universities and some government agencies.

Configuring Windows for the Internet

Before you can get on the Internet, you have to give Windows all the information it needs to make this Internet thing work.

Your ISP should provide you with *all* of the following information when you sign up:

✔ The phone number to call to log on to the Internet.

✔ Your ISP's domain name, which looks like this: `something.com` or `something.net`.

✔ Your Internet login ID and password.

✔ The number for your provider's DNS (Domain Name Server). This is a four-part number separated by periods, like this: `123.456.789.0`.

✔ The name of your ISP's e-mail server, which involves an acronym such as POP3 or SMTP.

✔ Your Internet e-mail name, address, and password (which is different from your Internet login password).

✔ The name of your ISP's news (NNTP) server.

Now you have all the information you need to configure Windows for the Internet. You can use the Internet Connection Wizard, which comes with Windows, to handle the configuration for you. You simply start the wizard, give it the information you just recorded, and it does the rest.

Follow these steps to start the Internet Connection Wizard:

1. Click the Start button.

2. Choose Programs.

3. Choose Internet Explorer.

4. Choose Connection Wizard.

5. Work through the wizard, and answer the questions using information provided by your ISP.

6. Click the Finish button at the end of the wizard.

After you run the wizard, you can see a new folder in the My Computer window: Dial-Up Networking. This folder contains the icon that you can use to connect to the Internet. However, if you're running Windows 98 and using Microsoft's Internet Explorer, the connection is automatic.

If your Internet Connection Wizard doesn't run automatically, you can find it in a variety of places, depending on how your computer is set up and what version of Windows you have. Try these paths: Programs⇨Accessories⇨Internet Tools⇨Connection Wizard. Or Programs⇨Accessories⇨Communications⇨Internet Connection Wizard. Or Programs⇨Internet Explorer⇨Internet Connection Wizard. Don't you just love the way Windows stays consistent? Geez.

In Windows 95, the Internet Connection Wizard could be here: Programs⇨Internet⇨Get on the Internet. Or you may just want to run the disk given to you by your ISP, which connects you automatically.

Never throw out any information your ISP gives you. You may need those numbers later.

Connecting to the Internet

After you connect with the ISP's computer, your computer is "on" the Internet. Connecting to the Internet is actually a combination of two things happening. First, your PC dials up the ISP. Then you use Internet software to access information on the Internet.

Follow these steps to connect to the Internet:

1. Click the Start button.

2. Choose Programs.

3. Choose Internet Explorer. These steps start your Web browser, but you can also just double-click the Internet Explorer icon located on your desktop.

4. Fill in any missing information in the Connection dialog box (if it appears). After the Internet software starts, you may see the Connect To dialog box.

5. Enter your Internet user name and password if you see a dialog box where this is requested. You can click the Save Password box to save you the trouble of typing the password each time you log on.

6. Click the Connect button to direct your modem to dial. (This may be optional if you've configured Windows to connect automatically.) Your computer connects to the Internet.

After you're connected, you may see the Connection Established dialog box. You can just close the box.

Remember: If your computer has an external modem, be sure that it's turned on before you dial.

E-Mail

E-mail is nothing more than an electronic postal service — it's electronic mail (hence, *e-mail*). And you can't do e-mail unless you're connected to the Internet.

Beginning the e-mail program

Outlook Express is the e-mail program provided by Windows. To begin Outlook Express, simply double-click the Outlook Express icon sitting on the desktop.

You see the following after you open Outlook Express:

- **Folder list:** In the upper left of the window is the list of folders where sent, received, trashed, and filed mail is stored.

- **Contact list:** In the bottom left is a list of contacts — people with whom you normally communicate.

- **Message summary:** On the right is a "home page" of sorts for messages, newsgroups, and so on. You may or may not see this screen depending on how your e-mail is set up and whether or not you've asked to be notified of newsgroup information. This is the kind of stuff you eventually get after you've played around with e-mail, signed up for newsgroups, and gotten your feet wet a little.

Sending e-mail

Follow these steps to send an e-mail message:

1. With Outlook Express now open (you just opened it in the preceding steps), click the New Mail button.

2. Type an e-mail address in the To field. *Remember:* E-mail addresses do not contain any spaces.

3. Type the message's subject in the Subject field.

4. Type a message in the New Message window. You need to click your mouse there first to get your cursor in the right spot.

5. Click the Send button. The message flies off into cyberspace, headed for the address you indicated in the To field.

Reading e-mail

To read a message, click the message. The message text appears in the bottom of the window.

To read another message, select it from the list. Selecting a new message displays its contents in the bottom part of the window.

After reading a message, you can print, reply, forward, delete, or stow the message.

Printing an e-mail message

People print e-mail messages more often than you think. Someone e-mails you directions to their house. You can print the directions and take them with you. Your boyfriend writes you a nasty message, so you print that and hand it to him, asking him what exactly he meant. Yes, printed e-mail messages can be of great help.

To print e-mail messages, you have to be in your e-mail program (Outlook Express in this example). You also need to have the e-mail message opened, as if you were reading it right then and decided to print it.

Follow these steps to print an e-mail message while in Outlook Express:

1. Choose File from the menu bar.

2. Choose Print. The Print dialog box appears.

3. Click OK to print.

You can also print an e-mail message by clicking the Print button on the toolbar or pressing Ctrl+P.

Replying to an e-mail message

Follow these steps to send an answer to an e-mail message:

1. In Outlook Express, open the e-mail message that you want to reply to.

2. Click the Reply button. You can also use the keyboard shortcut, Ctrl+R. A message composing window appears, similar to the New Message window. The sender's name is automatically placed in the To field. Your reply goes back directly to the sender without you having to retype the address.

3. Type your reply in the message composing window.

4. Click the Send button to send off the reply.

Deleting an e-mail message

To delete the message that you're reading in your e-mail program (and we're talking about Outlook Express here), click the Delete button. The deleted message is moved into the Deleted Items folder on the left side of the Outlook Express window. The deleted mail sits in the Deleted Items folder until you clean out that folder.

Follow these steps to clean out the deleted folder:

1. Choose Edit from the menu bar.

2. Choose Empty Deleted Items Folder from the menu. Your folder is gone for good.

Attaching a file

E-mail really became exciting when folks discovered that you could do more than write cute notes: You could also send people pictures and documents. For example, I sent the chapters of this book to my editor via e-mail.

To attach any file to an e-mail message, start by writing a message just as you normally would. Then "paper clip" the file to your message. The file you attach can be a Word document, a picture — anything that you can create on your computer.

Follow these steps to attach a document to an e-mail:

1. Create the file that you want to send. Do this ahead of time. After all, you need something to attach.

2. Start Outlook Express. You can do this by double-clicking the Outlook Express icon on your desktop. If you can't find that icon, you can take the long way around by choosing Start⇨ Programs⇨Microsoft Outlook.

3. Compose your e-mail message. Decide who you're sending your stuff to. Then have the To: box complete, the subject line filled in, and write a little note explaining what you're attaching.

4. Click the paper clip icon that has the word Attach under it.

5. Find the file that you want to attach by searching through the Look in area. You may have to click around until you find it.

6. Click the file once to select it.

7. Click Open. The file is attached to your e-mail message.

8. Press the Send button. Your e-mail message and the attachment are whisked off through the Internet.

Creating a mail folder

While in Outlook Express, I make specific folders for my e-mail so that I can keep them or refer to them later. I have a Funny folder for the jokes that actually make me laugh. I have a Picture folder for those adorable pictures that family members and friends send. I also have folders for Work, News, and so on.

Follow these steps to create a mail folder:

1. Choose File from the menu bar.

2. Choose New.

3. Choose Folder.

4. Type a name for the new folder.

5. Click the folder in which you want the new folder to be placed. If you choose the Local Folders item, the folder is placed on the main level. Choosing another folder creates a subfolder.

6. Click OK. The newly created folder now appears in the Folders list on the left side of the window.

Right-clicking these new folders produces a pop-up menu. Notice the commands for renaming and deleting in case you want to reorganize or clean house.

Follow these steps to view the contents of a folder:

1. Click to open the folder you want from the Folders list. The messages stored in this folder are listed on the left side of the window.

2. Click to open the message you want to read. After you've read a message, you can drag it to a folder just like you drag an icon. From the Inbox, for example, you can drag a message over to your Pictures folder. Just point the mouse at the envelope next to the message and drag it to the proper folder on the left side of the window.

You can delete messages by dragging them to the Deleted Items folder.

Keeping an Address Book

The Address Book in your e-mail program (Windows Outlook Express, for example) is similar to that little black book you keep in your hip pocket or your purse. This Address Book, however, holds your e-mail addresses. You can add an e-mail name to the Address Book in two ways: manually and automatically.

Adding a name to the Address Book manually

Follow these steps to add names to the Address Book manually while you're in Outlook Express:

1. Click File from the menu bar.

2. Choose New.

3. Choose Contact. This creates a new Address Book entry.

4. Fill in the boxes. You can put as little or as much information as you want. I suggest that you at least include the first name, last name, any nickname, and the e-mail address. The nickname is optional, but a friend listed my nickname as Queen of the Universe, and I love that.

5. Click the Add button.

6. Click OK. Your Address Book entry is safely stored.

You can click the Address Book button on the toolbar if you need to edit any of the addresses in your Address Book.

Adding a name to the Address Book automatically

You can have Outlook Express automatically add to your Address Book the e-mail address and name of those people you reply to with e-mail. That way, your Address Book isn't filled with addresses from the spam mail you may receive; instead, only the addresses of those people you care enough to respond to are entered in the Address Book.

Follow these steps to add people to your Address Book when you send them a reply by e-mail:

1. In Outlook Express, choose Tools from the menu bar.

2. Click Options.

3. Make sure that the Send tab is forward. Click the option Automatically Put People I Reply to in My Address Book.

Participating in Auctions on the Internet

I remember going to cattle auctions as a kid. The auctioneer would rattle off numbers like he was using a new language. Now you can participate in auctions online. They don't have auctioneers in the traditional sense, but the bidding process is much the same.

In most cases, the auctioneer is the Web page itself. It works like a combination search engine and online retailer.

The search engine lets you look up whatever item you're trying to buy. The seller offers a price, and you bid on it along with everyone else on the Internet who wants that same item. The price keeps going up until the bidding stops. The item goes to the highest bidder.

You may want to visit these popular auction sites:

✔ auctions.amazon.com

✔ auctions.yahoo.com

✔ www.ebay.com

Be prepared to pay a commission to the Web site if you are selling an item. This is how the online auction site makes its money.

Planning Trips on the Internet

The Web brings the world to your fingertips, which makes it an excellent travel agent.

Most Internet sites ask you some basic questions regarding your travel plans. So, to use the Internet to plan a trip, you have to make decisions before you even get on the Internet.

Here are some travel-planning points to consider:

✔ Decide where you want to go. The Internet requires you to be specific. To search for a place "warm and sunny with clear blue water" doesn't work.

✔ Decide when you want to go. The more flexible you are regarding dates, the more opportunity you have to save money. Resorts usually offer discounts during the "off" season.

✔ Determine how many people are going with you (kids, grandparents, one friend?). This information is for booking hotel rooms and your transportation.

✔ Decide how you want to travel: car, airplane, train, boat, horseback. All of them.

The exciting part of the Internet is that you have access to information about any place in the world. Many resorts also have Web sites where you can view the property and see pictures of their rooms, all from the comfort of your home.

The real downer about planning trips on the Internet is that this research takes a lot of time. Especially when it comes to the point when you're actually reserving airline tickets or rental cars. Use a search engine to research locations. Altavista.com is one of my favorites. Type `www.altavista.com` in the address line of the Internet Explorer program. Then in the search box of altavista.com, type a name of someplace you'd like to visit, such as Acapulco.

Read through the list of information and click on a resort that sounds fun, such as Las Brisas. Las Brisas is one of those resorts that lists their prices for you. Notice that there is an off-season section listing lower prices. (This may have something to do with the extreme heat in Mexico during the off season, which would prevent any sane person from going there. Then again, I could be wrong.)

Las Brisas is one of many hotels that gives you all kinds of information on its Web site, but you still have to call to reserve a room. This is when you need to know the number of people going with you and your length of stay.

Now you have to decide how you're going to get to your final destination. Again, this is where the Internet can be somewhat limiting because of the time involved.

Airline travel has really taken advantage of the Internet, and you can go to several places to find airline and rental car information. Here are just of few of those Internet sites:

- `travel.yahoo.com`
- `travelocity.com`
- `expedia.com`

Cruise lines post their scheduled trips, complete with dates, cruising locations, and costs, but most of the cruise lines want to personally speak with you. You still have to pick up the telephone and call them. Go to `www.princess.com` for a peek.

 If you're one of those people who flies with only one airline, you can go to that airline's Web page (such as `ual.com` for United Airlines and `alaskaair.com` for Alaska Airlines) and book your flight directly with them. This is usually a faster process because you have fewer options to choose from. You may also end up paying a higher price for your ticket.

Using the World Wide Web

The World Wide Web is composed of information — lots of different types of information. You can play games, shop, invest, and read if you like. It's all there. What you do with this information is up to you.

Finding things on the Web

To find something on the Web, you use a search engine. A search engine is a Web page that contains lists of other Web pages, sort of like a catalog. You search through these lists for whatever you're looking for, and the results (in the form of Web page links) are displayed on-screen. You can then click those links to get to the Web page that you want.

These search engines are the more popular ones, but, really, the list is nearly endless:

- http://ask.com
- www.dogpile.com
- http://excite.com
- www.goto.com
- www.hotbot.com
- http://search.com
- www.webcrawler.com
- www.yahoo.com

The following Web pages are search engines that you can use to find people or businesses:

- www.411locate.com
- www.bigfoot.com
- www.northernlight.com
- www.switchboard.com
- www.whowhere.lycos.com
- www.people.yahoo.com

Finding games online

I know. You never use your computer to play games. Yeah, right. If you decide that you *do* want to play games, you'll find two types of online games:

- **Games that run on a Web page:** You sign up, you're given a player or dealt a hand of cards. Then you play with other people all over the world. Playing them costs nothing more than your time.

- **Games for which you purchase software for your PC:** The game uses the Internet to connect with other people who are playing the same game.

Follow these steps to play an online game:

1. Find a game to play. You can go to `http://games.yahoo.com` to find some good ones.

2. Sign up for the game.

3. Download the game software to your PC. The Web site may ask if you want to download the software. If so, click OK.

4. Play the game.

Another good place to go for some fun online games is `www.won.net`.

Introducing MP3

The Internet is a hornet's nest of latest rages, and the latest and loudest of them all is the MP3 craze.

MP3 is the name of an audio format, one that stores lots of CD-quality music in a file that doesn't use much hard drive space and doesn't take forever to download. It's like an online music store, although virtually everything there is free.

You can find MP3 at this Web site: `www.mp3.com`

Follow these steps to download music files from the Internet to your computer:

1. Start Internet Explorer to connect to the Internet.

2. Visit `www.mp3.com`.

3. Find a link to the music that you want.

4. Click the link and download. You can browse the MP3 site for music, search the site, or click one of the links on the main page, such as the <u>Song of the Day</u> or the <u>Hot New MP3</u> titles. When you find a title that you'd like to hear, click that title. That takes you to a page where you can read more information and even download (save) the music file to your computer.

Follow these steps to save music to a file:

1. Right-click the link for the music file.

2. Choose Save Target <u>A</u>s from the shortcut menu. The Save As dialog box opens.

3. Browse this dialog box to find a disk drive and folder for the file. For example, perhaps you want to create a new MP3 folder in your My Documents folder.

4. Type a name for the file or use the one that is inserted automatically in the File Name text box.

5. Click the Save button. Now sit back and wait as the MP3 music file is sent from the MP3 Web page to your computer.

6. Close the dialog box after your music has been downloaded.

To play the music, double-click the file. Usually the music starts on its own. If it doesn't, just click the Play button (like the one on your CD player at home).

Saving and investing online

Many banks have online services or have started them in anticipation of the flood of interest in online banking.

The problem? At first, online banking was expensive. Extra charges were involved, and people had lots of hassles getting connected. For example, when I first got started with online banking, my bank charged a $25 start-up fee for online banking services, and then if I wanted to do anything other than check my balance, I had to phone the bank for verbal confirmation. That didn't seem very online to me.

Today's online banking is easier, thanks to the Web. Inquire with your bank or financial institution about online banking. Find out what's involved, what the fees are, and if the bank can work with financial software, such as Quicken or Microsoft Money. If you can pay your bills by having Quicken phone in the list of checks to print, it really makes online banking worthwhile.

Checking those stocks

In addition to online banking, you can also wheel and deal on the stock market online. Basically, you find an online trading service (or maybe your current broker offers such a service) and sign up. After you sign up, you can buy and sell stocks until you're broke — or until you retire to that island you bought in the Caribbean.

If you're not into wheeling and dealing, you can still use the Web to check your stock prices. Yahoo! and many other portal sites offer methods for checking stock quotes throughout the day. The following figure shows the Yahoo! Finance Web site (http://finance.yahoo.com), where you can check the market, read financial news, or look up stock quotes.

By the way, I do not own any stock in Yahoo!, even though I tend to recommend it a lot. (Just being fair.)

Shopping online

Do you want to be really hip? Shop online! You can buy computers, books, clothes, knick-knacks — even real estate — from the comfort of your home. All you need is a credit card number.

Follow these steps to shop online:

1. Decide what you want to buy.

2. Find a Web page that sells what you want to buy. Amazon.com is one of my favorites. It started as an online bookstore but now sells other goodies as well. You can get there by typing www.amazon.com on the address line of your Web browser.

3. When you find what you want, review the information.

4. Pick out a product and add it to your virtual shopping cart by clicking a button. The item is placed into a "bin" until you're ready to check out later.

5. Pay for the item. The check-out process is different for each store, but the online store usually makes things fairly simple. Follow the instructions on the screen to check out, which usually involves filling in personal and shipping information, as well as a credit card number.

The biggest question for most online shoppers regards the safety of their credit card information. Most shopping sites and Web browsers use special encryption technology to ensure that no one steals credit card numbers. Believe it or not, this is much safer than handing your credit card to a waiter in a restaurant.

It's impossible to list all the stores available online. And rather than list all my favorites, go to one of the search engines to find your favorite store's Web site. Type the name of your favorite store, such as Nordstrom's, and the Nordstrom Web site is listed. Click the appropriate link and go shopping!

Always check the store's return policy! Some places are quick to accept returns. If possible, try to find a place that has a no-questions-asked return policy. But watch out! Some places are cryptic and hide return information. Always check!

Signing off the Internet

Follow these steps to exit the Internet:

1. Quit all your Internet programs.

2. A dialog box is displayed asking whether you want to disconnect from the Internet.

3. Click the Disconnect button. If a Disconnect dialog box doesn't appear, such as when you want to keep a window or two open (like a Web page), you must "manually" disconnect. To do this, double-click the Connected To icon in the system tray. A window appears. Click the Disconnect button and you're finished.

The system tray is located at the bottom right of your screen, next to the time.

Maintaining Your Computer

You store applications and all the data and documents that you create on disk drives. Throughout this book, and pretty much in any computer book you read, this is refered to as *saving to disk*. When you are told to "click the save button," that information is being saved on a disk drive.

Much of what you do inWindows deals with disks, so they are central to your PC's operation. If you've paid for one of those speedy computers, maintaining the disk drive keeps it speedy. Ignoring your disk drive slows your computer to a painfully slow crawl. Therefore, keeping them happy and healthy is important.

In this part, I tell you some of the things that you can do to minimize your risk of PC problems.

In this part . . .

Backing Up Your Hard Drive

Backing up your hard drive is underrated. You need a backup copy in case something bad happens — for example, if a file is mangled or overwritten, if you lose a file that was there yesterday, a severe system failure, a hard drive crash that doesn't allow you to access your data, or worse yet — if someone reformats your hard drive.

What to back up and when to do it

You should have a backup schedule that works like this:

✔ Every week, back up your entire hard drive.

✔ Back up the work you do every day.

The first, and most important backup, is a full backup. This takes some time, but it keeps that valuable second copy of your information current.

The second backup is called an incremental backup. It backs up only those files that have been changed or created since the last time you did a full backup.

How to back up

Whether it's a daily backup or a weekly backup, you follow the same steps. Because I don't know exactly what you're backing up, I give you a fairly generic procedure here. Also, the following steps are for those using a tape backup system, which I highly recommend. You can use a floppy disk or Zip drive to back up, but the tape backup systems have the room to accommodate all the information on your hard drive without continually exchanging disks, which you would definitely have to do if you use floppy disks to back up your computer.

Don't start your backup until you're ready to go to bed. Yes, your computer can work while you sleep. When you start your backup, you are locked out of your computer until it's finished. This backup process can take lots of time — as in hours!

Follow these steps to back up your computer:

1. Close all open applications and then double-click the My Computer icon on the desktop.

2. Right-click a disk drive, such as drive (C:).

3. Choose Properties from the shortcut menu.

4. Click the Tools tab to bring that panel forward.

5. Click the Backup Now button.

6. Read the Welcome screen, Welcome to Windows 98 Backup!

7. At this point, your course takes one of two paths:

If you haven't performed a backup before: Make sure that a dot appears next to Create a New Backup Job. Click OK to start the Backup Wizard and go to Step 8.

If you have performed a backup before and created a backup job: Choose Open an Existing Backup Job. Pick your weekly or daily backup regimen from the window and click OK. Move on to Step 15.

8. In the Backup Wizard, choose Back Up My Computer (Back up all files and folders on my local drives).

9. Click Next.

10. Make sure that the All Selected Files option is chosen and click Next.

11. Choose your tape drive from the Where to Back Up drop-down list. (You should have a tape drive if you choose the tape drive option. If you don't, Windows doesn't back up your computer.)

12. Tell the Backup Wizard that you *do* want the backup system to compare the files to verify that the job was done successfully, and that you *do* want the files compressed to save space; then click Next.

13. Name your backup job; because you're backing up the entire hard drive — a full backup — call it Weekly or Monthly or however often you plan to do this.

14. Review the information that appears in the box in the middle of your screen; this confirms what you have selected. If there's something there that you don't like, click the Back button and do it over. When all the information is correct, move on to Step 15.

15. Click the Start button. Your computer is now being backed up.

16. Switch tapes as necessary (that is, when the computer tells you to). This isn't always necessary for every backup. So don't be surprised if you're never asked this. Also, if you start this at bedtime, this question is still there when you get up in the morning.

17. You're done (eventually!).

18. Remove your backup tape, label it, and keep it in a safe place.

19. Close the various windows to back yourself out of the Backup program.

Restoring something that you backed up

Backing up is pretty much useless without its counterpart, Restore. You use Restore to take the files stored on backup tapes and recopy them to your hard drive.

Backing up your computer literally takes the information on your hard drive, compresses the information, and stores it on the backup tape. Restoring is the process of taking this compressed information, uncompressing it, and putting it back on your computer. Kind of like what the transporter on *Star Trek* does with people.

Follow these steps to restore files from your backup tape or disk:

1. Start the Backup program. **See also** "How to back up" earlier in this part.

2. Choose Restore Backed Up Files.

3. Click OK and the Restore Wizard begins.

4. Put your first backup tape into the proper PC orifice. Kee-lunk!

5. Choose the proper backup device from the Restore Wizard program.

6. Click Next, and the Restore program scans your backup tape for a catalog of files.

7. Choose the *backup set* from which you want to restore files. It's probably the most recent set. If you're restoring only one file, you may need to choose a specific set. Click that set to put a check mark in its box.

8. Click the OK button and wait while the catalog (a list of files stored on the backup tape) is created. If your backup required more than one tape, you're asked to insert the next tape.

9. The list of files appears in the Restore Wizard window so that you can select the ones you want to restore. Similar to when you're backing up, you choose the files by working through the collapsible tree structure and placing a check mark beside all those files that you want to restore. To restore the entire hard drive, put a check mark in its box.

10. Click Next and choose where you want to restore the files. You have two choices: the Original Location or an Alternative Location. For full backups, or any time that you're recovering lost data, choose Original Location from the drop-down list. For recovering older versions of files, you may want to choose Alternative Location. That way, you can specify in the drop-down list where you want the files copied.

11. Click Next. You are asked whether you want to replace newer files with older ones on the backup tape? My advice is to choose Do Not Replace the File on My Computer.

12. Click the Start Restore button. Windows asks you to insert the first backup tape (even if you haven't removed it). Do so, if necessary.

13. Click OK.

14. Windows restores the files from your backup copy to your hard drive.

15. Swap tapes if necessary.

16. You're finished. Operation completed? OK! Close the various windows to back yourself out of the Backup program.

Defragmenting Your Hard Drive

Windows does some weird things to get information stored on your hard drive. To make room for all your files, Windows often takes advantage of empty spaces on the hard drive. Windows takes a file and splits it up — fragmenting the file into pieces that can fit into smaller, empty spaces on the hard drive. When you want to access a file that is stored in pieces like this, the reassembling takes time, which results in a sluggish computer.

When a drive has more than ten percent of its files fragmented, you should run the Disk Defragmenter tool. This is a special disk utility that puts fragmented files back together. You were once able to see how much of your files were fragmented, but Windows deleted that option with Windows 98. However, the option is back with Windows 2000. Because Microsoft is messing with our minds and won't be consistent, I recommend that you run the disk defragmenter once a month.

Follow these steps to run Disk Defragmenter:

1. Close all open documents and programs.

2. Double-click the My Computer icon on the desktop.

3. Right-click drive (C:) (or whatever drive you want to defragment).

4. Choose Properties from the shortcut menu.

5. Click the Tools tab to bring that panel forward.

6. Click Defragment Now. Windows starts working to defragment Drive C, which can be a rather boring process to watch. A dialog box appears to tell you when defragmentation is complete.

7. Click View Report. This isn't a necessary step, but the numbers are there for you to review.

8. Click Print, Save As, or Close. You don't have to save or print this report, but you can if you want to compare your reports.

9. Click the Close button, and you're finished.

 You can also reach the Disk Defragmentation box by clicking the Start button, choosing Programs⇨Accessories⇨System Tools, and then clicking Disk Defragmenter.

 The defragmentation process can take an hour or longer to complete. Don't start this process if you don't have the time to wait for it to finish.

Deleting Temporary Files

Disk drives don't exactly get dirty, but they do accumulate lots of junk files. You accumulate all sorts of temporary files when you browse the Web, and all that junk takes up space. You need to use the Disk Cleanup tool to get back all that precious hard drive space.

Follow these steps to run Disk Cleanup:

1. Click the Start button.

2. Choose Programs.

3. Choose Accessories.

4. Choose System Tools.

5. Choose Disk Cleanup.

6. Select the drive that you want to clean. You can click the down arrow to choose from the list of drives available.

7. Click OK. The Disk Cleanup for your disk drive shows you how much disk space you can clean up by running this program.

8. Click the files that you want to delete.

9. Click OK. The files you marked are deleted.

Remember: You should run Disk Cleanup every month or so.

Running ScanDisk

For some reason, files get lost or bits and pieces of them disappear, which seems to happen randomly and at unpredictable times. Fortunately, Windows has a tool called ScanDisk that you can use to fix these minor file boo-boos.

Follow these steps to run ScanDisk:

1. Open the My Computer icon on the desktop.

2. Right-click drive (C:) or whatever drive you want to defragment.

3. Choose Properties from the shortcut menu. This displays the Drive_(C:) Properties dialog box (or the dialog box for whatever drive you choose).

4. Click the Tools tab to bring that panel forward.

5. Click the Check Now button in the Error-Checking Status section of the Tools tab.

6. In the dialog box that appears, choose the type of test that you want to run: Standard or Thorough. Standard is automatically checked and typically works well.

7. Click Start and ScanDisk fires up. Very little really happens at this point. A small box is shown with a thermometer going across the screen (also known as a progress bar) to show you how long until the process is complete. When the disk check is complete, the ScanDisk Results window appears, providing the drive statistics.

8. Click Close to make the Results dialog box disappear.

9. Click Close to close the ScanDisk program

10. Click Close again to close the Drive (C:) Properties dialog box.

You should run Scandisk at least once a week — more often if your hard drives are particularly fussy (that is, they tend to freeze often or take a while to open your documents).

Scheduling Disk Maintenance

Using all the Windows disk maintenance tools is necessary to keep your computer operating at the best possible level of performance. It's part of using a computer, but a part that most people tend to neglect.

The Scheduled Tasks utility program is designed to automatically start various routine disk operations so that you don't have to remember to do them yourself. Just tell the Scheduled Tasks program what you want done and when you what it to happen.

Follow these steps to schedule disk maintenance:

1. Click the Start button.

2. Choose Programs.

3. Choose Accessories.

4. Choose System Tools.

5. Choose Scheduled Tasks. The Scheduled Tasks dialog box appears.

6. Double-click Add Scheduled Task. This starts the Scheduled Task Wizard. The next few steps walk you through choosing the tasks that you want to run and the times you want to run them. Sounds easy enough.

7. Click Next.

8. Find an appropriate task. You can look in two different places. One place to look is from the column called Applications; the second is to click the Browse button and find the program you want to schedule.

9. Choose Disk Defragmenter from the application list (or any other task that you want to schedule). But don't forget to go back and add other items.

10. Click Next.

11. Select when you want this to happen by clicking the dots beside the time you want the task to run.

12. Click Next.

13. Choose the month(s) and time when you want to run this task. These dialog boxes may look different depending on the time and the program you choose.

14. Click Next.

15. Read the notice displayed by your computer: `You have successfully scheduled the following task`, and then review the summary of your scheduling decisions that appears on-screen. If you want to change anything listed, click the Back button and rework that option.

16. Click Finish. An icon is listed, along with the scheduled time of the task, in the Scheduled Tasks dialog box.

You want to pick a time when you're not doing anything with the computer to run scheduled tasks. You don't want to be in the middle of work when your computer starts running ScanDisk, for example. Choosing 2 a.m. to run these programs is fine. Just remember that you have to leave your computer on for this to work.

With all the disk cleanup and maintenance stuff that Windows provides, knowing when, where, and how often to do this stuff can be confusing. The following table lists the clean up programs and when you should use them.

Program	Scheduled Time
Disk Cleanup	Once a week
Disk Defragmentation	Once a month
ScanDisk	Every week
Backup	Every week; daily if you change information often

System Information

Tech support people can be real nags. They tend to want to know things such as the make and model of your computer, how much memory you have, and what kind of hardware you have. You can find all this stuff in a place called System Information.

Follow these steps to find System Information:

1. Click the Start button.

2. Choose Programs.

3. Choose Accessories.

4. Choose System Tools.

5. Choose System Information.

The process of reviewing this information is similar to working with Windows Explorer. Click a plus sign (+) to open more folders and watch the information unfold on the right. You may not be able to interpret much of the information (all those numbers and such), but a tech support person will love you!

Part XI

Adding Gadgets to Your Computer

Peripherals are the extras that you can add to a PC to make it more useful (or more fun!).

A computer peripheral is any accessory or auxiliary piece of equipment you buy that is outside the main computer system. Examples of computer peripheral items include scanners, tape drives, CD-RWs, digital cameras, video cameras, and sometimes modems.

In this part . . .

About Peripherals

The most popular PC peripheral today is the scanner, although the digital camera is quickly gaining popularity. These toys have dropped in price over the past few years, making them even more accessible.

The rest of this section talks about peripherals that you can add to your computer. However, you can find information about modems and display adapters in a separate section later in this part.

CD-RW

You use rewritable CDs to store information, just as you would store information on a floppy disk. Like a floppy disk, you can also erase the information on a CD-RW and write new information to the disc.

To take advantage of this technology, you need a CD-RW drive, and you have to buy special CD-RW discs that typically hold about 650MB of memory. Then you can write and save to the disc until it's full. Basically, you're making your own CDs. The CD-RW hardware comes with software (a driver) that you have to install before you can use the drive.

Digital cameras

The digital camera is *the* hip toy to have. The images they take are often excellent, and their plunging prices make them much more affordable. They range in price from a few hundred to several thousand dollars.

Look for these two things in a digital camera:

- ✔ **Resolution:** Don't get anything with a resolution less than 1024x768 pixels. The average resolution is about 1280x1024, and some of the really nice digital cameras have a resolution of 1600x1200 pixels.

- ✔ **The number of photographs the camera can store:** This number varies from a few dozen to nearly 200. An interesting thing to note, however, is that you can delete images to make room for more. The camera is like a computer, so if you don't like one shot, you can remove it and try again. (Or if you take that embarrassing picture of your spouse, you can safely delete it later to avoid sleeping on the couch.)

Beware of digital cameras with too many dials and buttons. Those are the high-end models, suited for professionals.

DVDs

DVDs are fast becoming the standard for computer hardware. DVD discs are capable of storing up to 17GB of information on a two-sided disc. And then, of course, if you have a DVD drive on your computer, you can watch the movies that are, with increasing frequency, becoming available in DVD format.

Microphones

You probably don't *need* a microphone on your computer (at least not yet). Speech recognition software and Internet telephone set ups (both of which are still catching on) require a microphone; but other than that, you can live without one. Microphones are generally cheapy little gadgets that you can buy for under $20. Currently, there isn't much variety out there for microphones. Some monitors come with microphones built in, and some computer manufacturers ship microphones with their computers.

People who use the computer for professional tasks, like music mixing, would use a higher-end microphone with professional-level sound quality.

Modems

A modem is what connects your computer to the Internet. Many computers manufactured today have built-in modems, but if your computer is an older model, you may need to purchase one. *See also* the main "Modems" section later in this part for more information.

Scanners

Scanners work like photocopiers except the image is translated into a graphics image in your computer rather than copied onto paper. From there, you can modify the image, save it to disk, add it to a document, or send it as an e-mail attachment.

Follow these steps to scan an image:

1. Place an image (such as a picture) onto the scanner and close the lid.

2. Use your scanning software to grab the image. (The scanning software usually comes bundled with the scanner.)

Scanner trivia:

- Types of scanners: flatbed scanners, handheld scanners, and business-card scanners.

- Scanners can be used to "read" a document. This requires Optical Character Recognition (OCR) software.

- A handheld scanner looks like a miniature vacuum cleaner. You slide the scanner across a picture, and the picture appears on your screen.

- Scanners for home computers cost anywhere from $150 to nearly $1,000. The more you pay, the better the image quality.

- High-end, expensive scanners are usually used in the graphics industry.

- Try to get a single-pass scanner. They're faster than multiple-pass scanners.

- Don't bother with a SCSI scanner unless your PC has a SCSI port.

- If your PC has a USB port, get a USB scanner!

Sound cards

A sound card enables your computer to do three things:

- Play the recorded sounds you hear when you turn on the computer, run a program, or play a game. These are called wave sounds.

- Play music, such as from a music CD or from a MIDI file.

- Record your own voice — if you have a microphone and the proper software.

Tape backups

A tape drive is a device that you can use to store backups (copies) of all the information on your PC's hard drive. That backup copy serves as an emergency copy for those times — yes, it may happen — when your computer crashes and you lose all or part of your information.

Most PCs don't come with a tape backup unit. You have to purchase it and add it to your PC yourself. It's worth the price to do so.

Adding an external backup drive to your PC is simple. Basically, you plug it in and load the software to run it. Adding an internal drive, however, is a bit more complicated because you have to work inside the console. You may want to have a professional help you install an internal tape drive.

If you install a tape backup drive, be sure to use it regularly. Back up your work at least once a month. *See also* Part X for more information on backing up your information.

Video cameras

Video cameras are new PC toys. You can use them to record movies or single images, and you can now use your video camera to send live images over the Internet. It all depends on the software that comes with the camera.

A webcam is a video camera that is connected directly to a computer and sends pictures to the Web. For example, I have a webcam that takes pictures of my driveway and posts the pictures to my Web site. The webcam updates the Web site every thirty minutes.

 Make sure that the software you need is included with the camera. For example, video conferencing is only possible with the proper software. The camera is just a device — you need software to really play with it.

Evaluating Your Display Adapter

The display adapter is the internal part of a PC's video system. It's an expansion card that plugs into your PC's motherboard and gives your computer the ability to display text and graphics on the monitor.

Display adapters have features for artists, game players, and computer designers, and they come in a wide range of prices.

The measure of a display adapter is how much memory (video RAM) it has. Most adapters come with at least 1MB to 4MB of memory. The more expensive models are capable of up to 16MB. The more memory the display adapter has, the higher the resolutions it can support, and the more colors it can display at those higher resolutions.

If your PC has a DVD drive, you need a display adapter capable of producing the DVD image on the monitor. The display adapters typically have an S-video out port that lets you connect a TV to the computer for watching things on a larger screen.

Remember: Some high-resolution graphics systems are only applicable to certain kinds of software. Computer graphics, computer-aided design (CAD), animation, and design are all areas in which paying top dollar for your display is worth the cost. If you're using only basic applications, such as a word processor, you don't need an expensive display.

Installing Peripherals

Installing a peripheral means that you're telling your computer that you want to add new hardware to the system.

Adding hardware is fairly simple and requires two general steps:

1. Connect the peripheral to the proper hole in the back of the computer.

2. Plug the peripheral into the wall (assuming that the peripheral has an electrical cord).

Okay, there are a few more steps to complete before you can actually *use* your peripheral — such as telling Windows that a new piece of hardware is connected — but plugging the thing into the proper port is the most important. (Incidentally, I explain the remaining steps in the following section.)

In some cases, you may be required to open the console and plug the peripheral in, such as when you add an expansion card.

Turn off your computer whenever you install hardware inside of or plug peripherals into your PC. An exception is any USB device, which you can just plug in and go.

Telling Windows about a peripheral

Installing a peripheral involves two things: the hardware and the software. The hardware installation basically involves plugging in the peripheral. Software installation involves telling Windows about the peripheral.

Follow these steps to install the software:

1. Read the installation instructions provided with your new gadget and install the peripheral.

2. Restart your computer.

Magically, Windows recognizes the new hardware — thanks to the wonders of *Plug and Play* technology. You *plug* the hardware in and *play* with your new toy.

When Windows finds the new hardware, it adds special software, called a *driver*, to control the hardware. This software may be included on the Windows CD, or it may come on a floppy disk or CD packaged with the peripheral. There is a point in its dizzying search for a driver that Windows may ask if you have a disk. This can occur at any time. If you do, insert the disk (or CD) into the proper slot and follow the on-screen directions.

Check to see whether your PC sports a USB port. If it does, try to buy the USB version of whatever peripheral you're buying — speakers, joystick, scanner, whatever. USB hardware is the best and easiest to install.

Helping Windows recognize the peripheral

Windows may not recognize your new hardware. This rarely happens, but it does happen. It could be that the hardware isn't Plug and Play, or maybe whatever you're installing just doesn't grab the attention of Windows.

Follow these steps when Windows doesn't recognize new hardware:

1. Click the Start button.

2. Choose Settings.

3. Choose Control Panel.

4. Double-click the Add New Hardware icon. The Add New Hardware Wizard appears.

5. Follow the steps on-screen. Click the Next button, or choose options as necessary. Your new hardware should be up and running as soon as you work through the wizard.

Modems

A modem takes digital information from your computer and translates it into analog signals (sounds) that are sent over phone lines. Communications software is responsible for sending and receiving information using the modem. The communications software dials the modem, connects with another modem (wherever you tell it to go), and then gets the two computers to talk.

That's the techie explanation for a modem. For those of you who don't really care about what goes on behind the scenes, the part you do want to know is this: The modem enables your computer to talk to other computers, which in turn connects you to the Internet. So if you want to get connected to the Internet, you need a modem.

Internal modems fit inside your computer console, and external modems live in their own box outside your computer console. Models vary, with different speeds, features, brand names, and prices ranging from inexpensive to very expensive.

Modem speed

Modems come in different speeds. The faster the modem, the quicker you connect to wherever you call. This is an important factor to those who are frequently logging on to the Internet.

Modem speed is measured in bits per second *(bps)*, although the three speeds most common on modems today are actually measured in *Kbps*, or kilobits per second (one kilobit is a little more than 1,000 bits). The three most common modem speeds are 28.8 Kbps, 33.6 Kbps, and 57.6 Kbps.

✔ **28.8 Kbps:** The minimum speed for using the Internet

✔ **33.6 Kbps:** The second fastest speed

✔ **57.6 Kbps:** The fastest standard modem speed and a must for the serious Internet surfer

Faster speeds are available, but you need to use a nonstandard modem to get a faster speed (such as a cable modem).

The correct term to describe modem speed is *bps*. Please don't use the term *baud* because that just isn't correct.

Fax modem

With the proper software, most modems have the ability to send or receive a fax. A modem with this added function is known as a *fax modem*. A fax modem can communicate with other PCs, modems, and fax machines. The special software that Windows uses for its fax modem is called Microsoft Fax. If you bought your computer and it's already equipped with the ability to fax, you have Microsoft Fax.

Types of modems

Several different types of modems exist. The following list of modem options can help you choose the modem that's right for you:

✔ **Standard modem:** Regular, off-the-shelf modems that connect to your existing phone system. The speed directly relates to the price. A top speed of 57.6 Kbps can cost anywhere from $50 to $150, depending on the make and model.

✔ **Soft modem:** This type of modem works with the computer, which does all the processing. This means the modem can be upgraded using software. You no longer have to buy a new modem; you just upgrade the soft modem software, and you have a brand new modem.

✔ **Duo modem:** The duo modem is fast because it uses two phone lines at once. Of course, to use the duo modem, you need two phone lines and permission from your Internet Service Provider to log in two times at once.

✔ **ISDN modem:** A step up from the traditional modem, the ISDN model requires that you have ISDN service, which your phone company installs. (ISDN stands for Integrated Services Digital Network.)

✔ **ADSL modem:** The ADSL modem gives you fast access by using unused frequencies in the phone line. The big drawback to the ADSL modem is that you must be within a few miles of the phone company's main office to obtain the service. (ADSL stands for Asymmetric Digital Subscriber Line; it is sometimes abbreviated as DSL.)

✔ **Satellite modem:** The satellite modem is similar to the ADSL modem, except that you access it through a satellite. For a satellite modem, you need a satellite dish and subscription to the service. The satellite then sends information to your computer extremely fast. You do, however, still need a regular modem to send information to the Internet because the satellite modem is only for receiving information.

✔ **Cable modem:** The good news is that the cable modem is the fastest modem you can buy. The bad news is that you must live in an area serviced by a cable company that offers cable-modem access. The second piece of bad news is that as more people use cable modems at the same time as you, the overall speed of your modem decreases.

The following table is a comparison of modems, their prices, and their speeds:

Modem Type	Average Price	Speed (in bps)
Standard modem	$80	6K
Soft modem	$140	56K
Duo modem	$250	112K
ISDN modem	$300	128K up to 512K
Satellite modem	$300	512K
ASDL modem	$400	8,000K
Cable modem	$180	30,000K

Connecting your modem

Setting up a modem is fairly easy. The optimal situation is to give your modem its own phone line, so that you don't have to share with the house phone line. Most homes have the ability to have a second phone line. You may or may not have an additional cost depending on where you live.

You may want your own modem phone line because you can't use your phone (as a phone) when you use your modem. In some cases, picking up the phone line while the modem is in use disconnects the modem. Not to mention that everyone calling into your home either gets a busy signal or is put through to your voice mail, if you subscribe to that service.

Here are the basic differences between internal and external modems:

- ✔ **Internal Modem:** If your computer has an internal modem, all you have to do is connect a phone cable from the modem port on the back of the computer and plug the other end into the phone wall socket or phone jack, just like plugging in a phone. (Chances are this modem was already installed for you when you bought the computer — if not, get someone to install it for you.)

- ✔ **External Modem:** Anyone can connect an external modem (I tell you how in the following steps). It's fairly simple after you get a handle on the cables. And after it's all hooked up, you never have to mess with it again.

You should find four things to connect to the back of an external modem. The following figure shows them all, although they may look somewhat different on the back of your modem.

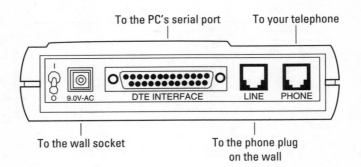

Follow these steps to install an external modem:

1. Plug one end of a serial cable into the rear of your PC. Plug the cable into either COM1 or COM2.

2. Plug the other end of the serial cable into the back of your modem.

3. Plug one end of the phone cord into the wall jack and the other end into the Line hole on the back of the modem. Notice that the connector snaps into place so that it won't accidentally unplug.

4. If you have a phone connected to the wall jack, plug it into the modem's Phone hole. That way, you can still use your

telephone when you're not using the modem. If you don't have a phone plugged into the wall here — if you plan to use only the modem on that line — you don't have to plug anything into the Phone hole.

5. Make sure that the modem is turned off while you're making these connections. The switch can be found either on the side or back of the modem.

6. Plug the power cord into the back of the modem, and plug the other end into a wall socket or power strip.

Familiarize yourself with the location of the modem's on/off switch. You should also find the volume control, which may be behind the modem or under one of its sides.

Remember: Don't forget to turn the modem's power on when you're ready to use it. Some people turn modems off after using them, although it's okay to leave your modem on all the time.

Telling Windows about your modem

After setting up your modem, you must tell Windows about it. Because your modem is a piece of hardware, you need to ensure that Windows recognizes your modem in order for it to work properly. *See also* "Installing Peripherals," earlier in this part for some suggestions on how to do this.

Modem solutions

Every now and then, Windows may lose track of the modem. This often happens right after you've reset or turned on your computer. No tricks await you here. You simply need to reset and see whether your modem is recognized.

Remember: Make sure that your external modem is turned on before you dial.

Upgrading

The computer world frequently offers updates and upgrades on hardware. Something newer and better is always coming along, and the computer industry is determined to convince you that you need it all.

What to buy first

Here's the big question: "Should I buy a new computer or upgrade my old one?" Here are some thoughts that may help you decide:

- ✔ **Memory:** Your first upgrading priority should be memory. It's not that expensive, and just about all your software works better with more memory. More memory also means that your computer can handle more graphics and sound.

- ✔ **Hard drive:** Most PCs can handle two hard drives, so buy a second hard drive — and make it a big one. If there's no room in your computer case for another hard drive, you can always buy an external hard drive or replace one of your current drives with a larger one.

- ✔ **Monitor:** Buy a big monitor — as in 21 inches big, if possible. You'll definitely be spoiled after you work on a big monitor.

- ✔ **Microprocessor:** Although upgrading your microprocessor is an option, it's not something that I recommend. It's just better to buy a whole new computer. That way you get *all* new components at a cost cheaper than buying a new PC one component at a time.

When to buy a new computer

You should replace your old computer every four or five years. Why then? By that time, the cost of a new system typically is cheaper than upgrading. If that seems too soon for you, evaluate the reasons why you bought your computer in the first place. If your computer still meets all your computing needs, you're fine, and you should upgrade only when you really need to. If you can't seem to get your work accomplished because your computer is too slow, doesn't have enough memory, or isn't compatible with someone you may need to share information with, you probably do need to break down and buy a new computer.

When to update Windows

Think carefully before you decide to update Windows. Everything in your computer relies on Windows, so performing an upgrade affects all the software in your computer. If you upgrade, your software may not work properly.

The bottom line? You don't need to upgrade Windows most of the time, especially if Windows is currently working well for you and all your software is working properly.

If, after a time, you notice that all the newer software packages work with the newest version of Windows, and this software is something you need, you may want to upgrade. But generally speaking, upgrading Windows is not necessary.

Troubleshooting

Even with the general computer help that books like this can provide, there still are times when you have questions about very specific problems. Handling those problems is called *troubleshooting*.

In this part, I try to help you become a better troubleshooter by helping you find the answers to some of the PC dilemmas you may encounter.

In this part . . .

Diagnosing Common Computer Problems

Whenever a computer starts acting up — the screen freezes, things become very slow, the screen starts looking weird — there are some things that you should do and check right away.

Checking your hardware

Always check your hardware first:

- Are all the cables connected? Did they wiggle loose?
- Is the monitor plugged in?
- Is the printer or modem plugged in and turned on?
- Is the keyboard and mouse cable plugged in tight?

Checking to see whether you have control of the computer

Computers, software, keyboards, mice — nothing seems to be happening at all. It's a fact of life.

When a program dies, you see an error message, you notice that things aren't working properly, or you don't get any response. If so, you need to determine how much control you still have over the PC.

- **Does the mouse still work?** If so, good. If not, try the keyboard.
- **Does the keyboard work?** Try popping up the Start menu in Windows by pressing Ctrl+Esc. Now press the Esc key to make the Start menu go away.

If you have no mouse or keyboard control, your only option is to reset the computer.

See also "The Big Picture" for more information on resetting your computer.

Resetting to fix oddities

Resetting is sometimes the only thing you can do to fix a frozen program or mouse problems (or anything odd that seems to be happening):

- If the mouse pointer is missing from the screen, reset.
- If Explorer dies, reset.
- If a program freezes, reset.

Running ScanDisk after resetting

You should consider running the ScanDisk program after your computer crashes and you have to reset. This program checks your hard drives for errors and ensures that the disk system is in working order. *See also* Part X to find out more about ScanDisk and other ways to maintain your system.

ScanDisk runs automatically if something happens and Windows shuts down incorrectly. For example, I often accidentally kick off my computer when I cross my legs, which causes Windows to shut down incorrectly. When I restart, ScanDisk automatically runs.

Getting out of a dead program

Sometimes a program dies right in the middle of what you're doing, and you need to get rid of the body (well, okay, get the program off the screen). A sure sign that a program is dead is when the screen freezes and nothing works.

Follow these steps to deal with a dead program:

1. Press Ctrl+Alt+Delete. This brings up the Close Program window.

```
┌─ Close Program ──────────────────────── ☒ ┐
│ Explorer                                    │
│ RoboBabe (not responding)                   │
│ Mobsync                                      │
│ Ezsmart                                      │
│ Hjdbman                                      │
│ Iowatch                                      │
│ Systray                                      │
│ Wmexe                                        │
│ Runner                                       │
│ Imgicon                                      │
│                                             │
│ WARNING: Pressing CTRL+ALT+DEL again will restart your │
│ computer. You will lose unsaved information in all programs │
│ that are running.                           │
│                                             │
│  [ End Task ]  [ Shut Down ]  [ Cancel ]    │
└─────────────────────────────────────────────┘
```

2. Look for any programs in the list that show the words *not responding* after the dead program's name.

3. Click that program's name. You can repeat this step if you find that more than one program is not responding.

4. Click the End Task button to end the program.

You should now save your work, shut down other applications that may be running, and reset your PC using the Shut Down method. *See also* "The Big Picture" for more information about shutting down your computer.

General Advice

My goal for this section is to help you keep your computer happy and working well. Here are some things you can try as soon as you begin noticing that your computer is acting kind of flaky.

Stop working on your computer when the computer starts bugging out, acting weird, or freezing up. Whatever! Here are some things to consider and try:

- ✔ Anytime a program crashes or something doesn't work right, save and shut down. Restart your PC. That generally fixes most problems.

- ✔ Don't be foolish and continue working on the system or even play a game — or you'll be sorry.

- ✔ If you're having disk troubles, try saving your file to disk, but also use the Save As command to save the file to another hard drive, floppy disk, or Zip disk.

- ✔ Programs that crash don't go away — their corpses clog up memory space. You need to reset your PC to get that memory back.

- ✔ Don't panic if you see the word *Illegal* displayed when you do something on your computer. Computer programmers use this term to mean something is wrong or not permitted. For example, putting a colon in a filename causes an illegal warning.

Making an Emergency Boot Disk

The emergency boot disk is probably the best diagnostic tool that you can create for your PC, although you may never use it. In fact, tech support people are probably the only ones who ever use an emergency boot disk. An emergency boot disk is a special disk, usually a floppy, that can be used to start the computer when the hard drive fails to respond. This disk is created by Windows during installation or can be created using a special system program.

Follow these steps to create an emergency boot disk:

1. Click the Start button.

2. Choose Settings.

3. Choose Control Panel.

4. Double-click the Add/Remove Programs icon.

5. Click the Startup Disk tab to bring the panel forward.

6. Click the Create Disk button and follow the directions on-screen.

7. Insert a floppy disk into drive A and click OK. The data on the floppy disk will be overwritten, so make sure that it doesn't contain any files that you need. You may need the original Windows CD for this operation; a dialog box tells you to grab the CD if you need it.

8. When the program finishes creating the disk — you see a message indicating that the program is finished — remove it from your floppy drive and label it *Emergency boot disk*. Put it away for safekeeping.

Don't forget to upgrade your boot disk when you upgrade your hardware or your operating system.

Running Troubleshooter

Troubleshooter is a program included in the Windows Help system that is designed to answer your questions regarding Windows.

Follow these steps to run Troubleshooter:

1. Click the Start button.

2. Choose Help.

3. Click the Index panel if it's not already selected.

4. Type **Trouble** in the text box.

5. Double-click the word *troubleshooting*.

6. Scroll through the list to find the troubleshooting topic specific to your needs.

7. Select a topic and click Display.

8. Follow the links and click dots in the proper circles to answer questions and work through Troubleshooter.

Troubleshooter isn't going to answer all your questions. You may have luck about half the time finding the kind of help you need.

Troubleshooting Mystery Ailments

It would be nice if your computer gave a sound or visual warning when something weird was going to happen. It doesn't. It's just not that thoughtful. So, if you wake up one morning and things are sluggish or freezing up, consider the following questions:

🗸 Did I add any new PC hardware recently?

🗸 Did I add any new software?

✔ Have I changed any software?

✔ Have I reset any Windows options?

✔ Did I uninstall anything?

Most likely, a change occurred that you have forgotten. Narrowing down what changed can help you fix things, or at least can help you lead the tech support people or your PC guru to the proper cure.

Using Safe Mode

Windows starts in what is known as *Safe mode* if it detects a major problem. Or you may need to restart in Safe mode because of something you've done when you were messing around — you changed your desktop to white: background, text, everything, for example — and you can't see what anything says. Starting in Safe mode means that Windows runs but it loads only those files necessary to run at the basic, no-frill operation. When it does load, you see it displayed in a low-resolution, low-color mode with the words "Safe mode" displayed on the desktop.

Follow these steps to use Safe mode:

1. Shut down the PC as you normally would by clicking the Start button to pop up the Start menu. If you can't see the Start button, you can press Ctrl+Esc to open it.

2. Choose Shut Down. Press *u* to access the Shut Down command if you can't see it. The Shut Down Windows dialog box opens.

3. Choose Restart. If you can't see the Shut Down Windows dialog box (and this option), press Alt+R to select the Restart option.

4. Click OK. Press the Enter key if you can't see the OK button.

5. Press and hold the Ctrl key as Windows restarts. (You may need to press the F8 key on some PCs.) A special Startup menu, similar to the following, appears.

```
Microsoft Windows 98 Startup menu

=====================================


   1. Normal

   2. Logged (\BOOTLOG.TXT)

   3. Safe mode

   4. Step-by-step confirmation
```

```
5. Command prompt only
6. Safe mode command prompt only

   Enter a choice:
```

6. Find the Safe mode option (number 3 in this example) and type that number next to `Enter a choice`.

7. Press Enter. Safe mode starts, and Windows loads only those files necessary to run Windows.

8. Now, fix your problem! Change your text back to black or shrink icons that were too big. Change whatever mess you got yourself into.

Normally you only need to use Safe Mode if you've messed with your computer so much that you can't "see" what's going on. Operations still work, but you just can't see anything. If you find that you've followed these steps and nothing has happened, you may need to just turn your computer off and restart it. This, of course, is the worst possible way to do it. But it's the only alternative you have to the above steps.

Viruses on the PC

Do you ever find yourself thinking, "Do I have a virus?" or "Could this be a virus?" Computer viruses do exist, and they can really mess up your computer.

A computer virus is a special kind of computer program that spreads by making copies of itself. It infects your programs and interferes with the normal operation of your PC.

The really nasty part of dealing with computer viruses is that they are man-made. Yes, a person intentionally designs a virus program, hoping to create chaos.

Where you can get a virus

You can get a virus in the following ways:

- ✓ **Downloading files from a Web page on the Internet:** Well-known Web pages, like those from Microsoft or IBM, typically aren't the problem. Web pages from unknown sources tend to be the problem.

- ✓ **Sharing floppy disks with others.** You can easily pick up a bug from their computer.

- ✓ **Running a program sent to you as an e-mail attachment.**

✔ **Running a program from a chat room.** You don't know who is in a chat room, so don't assume these people are going to be nice. They could send you an infected program, just to be mean.

✔ **Using stolen software from friends or coworkers.** Always buy your own software. If you install software that you personally didn't buy, that's considered stolen software.

✔ **Allowing others to use your PC.** You don't know what others may download or what disks they may stick in your computer.

Where you cannot get a virus

You cannot get a virus from any of the following sources:

✔ **Downloads:** Downloading a virus won't infect your computer. The virus must be a program that you run. If you download the file and don't run it, you're safe.

✔ **E-mail:** Reading plain, text only e-mail messages won't give your PC a virus.

✔ **Picture files:** Picture files cannot infect your PC. JPEGs, GIFs, or even more elaborate graphics file formats cannot infect your PC.

✔ **Retail software:** The new stuff sold in stores is not infected. However, I can't be so certain about used software sold in stores or software that has already been opened.

✔ **Well-known Web or FTP sites:** Web sites such as `shareware.com` or any widely used FTP site doesn't have infected software on it. These sites keep a tight hold on their software to keep it clean.

Remember: The only way you can get a virus on your PC is to *run* an infected program. If you don't run the program, you won't get the virus.

Antivirus software

Some jobs or personal work habits may require that you download programs or share floppy disks. If this is the case for you, you need special antivirus software because you don't want to pick up a nasty bug from your friends or coworkers. Antivirus software removes the virus from your PC and alerts you if it invades your computer again.

Antivirus software tends to slow down your PC. You may want to run the software first to scan for viruses, and then configure it so that it scans your system only when you start the PC.

Visit McAfee at `www.mcafee.com` for a sample antivirus program.

When Your PC Is Stuck in Diagnostic Mode

You need to manually set your computer back in Normal mode if it keeps starting in something that looks like a "diagnostic" mode. If your computer is in a diagnostic mode, the text looks rather blocky and computer-ish.

Follow these steps to put your computer back in Normal mode:

1. Click the Start button.

2. Choose Run.

3. Type **MSCONFIG** in the Run dialog box.

4. Press Enter. This runs the System Configuration Utility program.

5. Make sure that the item Normal Startup is selected in the General tab.

6. Click OK. You should now be back in Normal mode.

Part XIII

Having Fun with Your Computer

Computers were designed to get work accomplished — to calculate numbers, produce documents, and impress your boss. But somewhere along the way, some joker decided that we might as well have some fun with them.

Fun comes in the form of having the power to change the computer to fit your personal likes and dislikes. It's also about music, games, sounds, and making things look pretty. That's what having fun with your computer is all about.

In this part . . .

Changing the Desktop

You're not required to live with what you see right now on your desktop. Quite the contrary. You can change all kinds of things with little effort.

Adding colors to the display

The Settings panel in the Display Properties dialog box lets you tweak your monitor's color. You can have only so much color, and the Settings panel lets you see just how much you can get away with.

Follow these steps to change the color:

1. Click the Start button.

2. Choose Settings.

3. Choose Control Panel.

4. Double-click the Display icon.

5. Click the Settings tab to bring the panel forward.

6. In the Colors drop-down box, choose the number of colors — from 16 colors up to 16-bit or 32-bit, or whatever huge value it gives you.

7. Click the Apply button to save your change to the Colors box without closing the dialog box; click OK to save your change and exit the dialog box.

In this section, *colors* refers to the variety of colors available in the image. You can have 16 colors or 32 colors. If you choose 16 colors, you can have 16 different colors, but only 16.

Technically, the number of colors is referred to as the *bit depth*. The colors can be expressed as a *bit* number, and 256 colors equals 8 bits. Something that has an 8-bit color depth has 256 colors available:

16 colors = 4 bits

256 colors = 8 bits

64,000 colors = 16 bits (also called High Color in Windows)

Millions of colors = 32 bits (also called True Color in Windows)

You can also access the Display Properties dialog box by right-clicking anywhere on the desktop; then from the shortcut menu, choose Properties.

Making stuff larger

You can give yourself more desktop space and make the icons larger if you have a difficult time seeing what's on your desktop.

Follow these steps to make stuff larger:

1. Click the Start button.

2. Choose Settings.

3. Choose Control Panel.

4. Double-click the Display icon.

5. Click the Settings tab to bring it forward.

6. Adjust the amount of "real estate" you have on your screen by changing the setting in the Screen Area box. Right now, the setting is probably set to 1024 by 768 pixels. Move the bar back and forth with your mouse to see how it affects your screen in the sample box. If you don't like the changes, move the lever back to the 1024 by 768 pixels.

7. Click the Advanced button in the bottom-right corner. The Font Size box should now be visible, and Small Fonts may already be chosen.

8. Click the down arrow in the Font Size box. This brings down a list of font options.

9. Choose Large Fonts to make the fonts on your desktop larger and easier to read.

10. Click OK to save all your changes. Click Cancel if you want to leave your settings as they were.

Changing the desktop colors

Right now, your desktop probably has a simple blue background and your icon labels are written in white text. That's standard, but you don't have to keep it that way.

Follow these steps to change the desktop colors:

1. Click the Start button.

2. Choose Settings.

3. Choose Control Panel.

4. Double-click the Display icon.

5. Click the Appearance tab to bring the panel forward. What you see is probably the Windows Standard scheme. It's fine. But change is always good!

6. Make sure that Desktop is selected in the Item area.

7. Click the down arrow in the Scheme box. A whole list of options is available.

8. Click each option to see how things change in the display area. You can select separate items if you don't want to change the entire display.

9. Choose something from the Item area.

10. Play with the Color and Size boxes to design your own desktop appearance. Play around with the custom colors box, too.

11. Click OK when you're ready to keep what you've created.

12. Click Cancel if you're chicken and afraid of the results.

Don't give your font and desktop background the same color, or you won't be able to read your text. Always remember to have contrasting colors so that you can see boxes and words.

Remember: If you mess things up too badly, go back to the Scheme box and choose Windows Standard.

Changing screen savers

Screen savers keep a constant motion on your screen so that one image isn't burned into the screen forever. You don't have to have a screen saver — and it's unlikely that an image *will* be burned into your screen forever — but it is a nice kind of weird art thing.

Follow these steps to change your screen saver:

1. Click the Start button.

2. Choose Settings.

3. Choose Control Panel.

4. Double-click the Display icon.

5. Click the Screen Saver tab to bring the panel forward.

6. Click the down arrow in the Screen Saver box.

7. Click an option from the list. The small computer screen shows you what the screen saver looks like.

8. Click the Preview button. This gives you the true effect by showing the screen saver all over your screen.

9. Wiggle your mouse to take you back to the Screen Saver panel.

10. From the Screen Saver drop-down list, choose another screen saver.

11. Click the Settings button. A dialog box is displayed in which you can adjust several things — color, pattern, speed, and so on.

12. In the Wait box, choose the amount of time you want Windows to wait before starting the screen saver. You can either type a number in the box or use the spinner controls (the small up and down arrows) to select the number of minutes. There's no right or wrong answer here.

13. Click OK when you're ready to move on and save your changes or click Cancel if you want to leave things alone.

Changing the wallpaper

You've seen computers that have pretty pictures on the desktop. What that computer user has done is changed the desktop *wall-paper* (also known as a *background*).

Follow these steps to change the desktop wallpaper:

1. Click the Start button.

2. Choose Settings.

3. Choose Control Panel.

4. Double-click the Display icon.

5. Click the Background tab to bring the panel forward.

6. Click one of the wallpaper options to view it in the small monitor. You can use the up and down arrows to view all your choices.

7. In the Display drop-down box, click the down arrow and choose the Center or Tile option to see how it affects your choice.

8. Click OK after you pick your new wallpaper.

Changing the way the monitor looks

Brightness and contrast of the monitor and size and placement of the image on your screen are controlled by a row of buttons somewhere at the bottom of your monitor. They may look similar to the buttons shown in the following figure. The buttons on your monitor may even be hidden behind a secret panel.

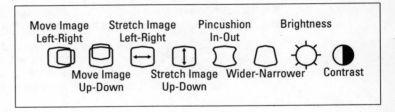

Move Image Left-Right Stretch Image Left-Right Pincushion In-Out Brightness

Move Image Up-Down Stretch Image Up-Down Wider-Narrower Contrast

Some monitors (usually the older models) use only a few buttons. Others have a whole slew of buttons, some with plus (+) and minus (–) buttons next to each aspect of the display.

Press the left-right, up-down, and stretch buttons to adjust the monitor's image to fill the screen.

Character Map Program

Windows not only provides you with some interesting fonts, but it also gives you a nice array of amazing characters. For example, locate the Wingdings icon in the Fonts folder. The Fonts folder can be found by clicking Start⇨Settings⇨Control Panel⇨Fonts. The preview window shows you many of the delightful characters in this decorative font, but you can't select the character in the window; and if you could, there's no Copy command available. Drat!

Thank heaven for the Character Map program. Not only does it preview all the characters in a font, it lets you copy and paste them into your documents.

Follow these steps to use the Character Map program:

1. Click the Start button.

2. Choose Programs.

3. Choose Accessories.

4. Choose System Tools.

5. Choose Character Map.

6. Choose Wingdings from the Font drop-down list. All the characters in the Wingdings font appear in the Character Map grid.

7. Aim the mouse pointer at a character and press and hold down the mouse button. The character you point at is magnified so that you can see it better.

8. Double-click one of the characters to make that character appear in the Characters to Copy text box. For example, the smiley character is a popular character to use. You can continue to double-click additional characters to add to the Characters to Copy text box, if you like.

9. Click Copy. The smiley character is copied to the Windows clipboard.

10. Click Close. Now you can open any program, such as Microsoft Word or WordPad, and paste the character into a document.

   See also Part III for information on copying and pasting text.

Getting Sounds from the Internet

Windows comes with a few interesting sounds, but really, they aren't nearly enough.

The easiest way to get a new sound is to search for sound files on the Internet. Use any popular search engine — look for *sounds* or *Windows sounds* — to find plenty of Web pages with sounds that you can download. And there are plenty of popular themes available, such as the Sandra Bullock Theme Page, Natalie Portman, and South Park. Geez, lots of stuff is out there.

Follow these steps to save sounds from the Internet:

1. Find a sound file that you want to save.

2. Right-click the link. (You may need to do lots of reading here. Web pages can differ in the way that sounds are listed. You may need to alter these steps based on what you find.)

3. Choose the Save Target As option.

4. Choose the C:\Windows\Media folder as the folder to save the sound files into. If you save the sound files in this folder, they appear in the Sounds and Multimedia dialog box.

5. Type a name for the sound (or use the one that is supplied), and click OK.

6. Click OK when you see the Download Complete notice.

You can also save sound files in your personal C:\My Documents\ Sounds folder.

Online Games

Popular computer games, such as Quake or Duke Nukem, can be taken online to play against others via the Internet. Each game accesses the Internet differently. These steps are basic to most online games:

1. Connect to the Internet.

2. Find a game server. The Internet has several specific places where you can log into a game server.

3. Run the game software. The server connects you with other players on the Internet.

4. Play the game.

You can do a team game in which you pair up with others to battle some element. Many games also feature the popular "death match" mode in which it's a free-for-all, and the last person standing wins.

Getting any more specific is difficult because each game plays differently. Most games do a good job of explaining the procedures.

Here are a couple of places to go for games:

✔ www.games.yahoo.com

✔ www.won.net

See also Part IX for more about accessing games over the Internet.

Downloading games

Because Windows doesn't supply you with anywhere close to an adequate number of games, you can download more from the Internet. You just find a game on the Internet and then transfer that game to your computer. All you need is the location of the file on the Internet and the time to download it on your computer.

You must be connected to the Internet to make any of this downloading jargon work. *See also* Part IX to find out how to access the Internet.

As with finding anything on the Internet, to find files for downloading you need a search engine, such as altavista.com. In this case, what you need is a file-finding search engine. There are many of them.

My favorite places to look for files are the following sites:

✔ www.filemine.com — File Mine

✔ `www.download.com` — Cnet's Download.com

✔ `www.jumbo.com` — Jumbo!

You can find more sites by using Yahoo! Go to `www.Yahoo.com` and click the <u>Computers and Internet</u> link, the <u>Software</u> link, the <u>Shareware</u> link, and, finally, the <u>Games</u> link.

Most file-finding engines have a main page that contains the following elements:

✔ **A search engine:** You type in the name of the program you're looking for, or a topic, such as **card games.**

✔ **A list of topics:** You can browse for software by various categories listed on the page.

✔ **A list of top downloads:** This lists the most popular downloads.

✔ **Featured items:** Sometimes, these are suggestions for neat and overlooked stuff.

✔ **Necessary items:** A good downloading Web page can also highlight some common tools that every computer user should have.

Follow these steps to download a game:

1. Double-click the Internet Explorer icon on your desktop to get onto the Internet.

2. Go to the Address line on Internet Explorer and type the name of a games site you found earlier using a search engine (**FileMine.com**, for example).

3. Press Enter.

4. Type the name of a game you want to download (for example, **blackjack**) into the Search dialog box. Make sure that the proper operating system is chosen.

5. Click the Search button. If you're lucky and your game is found, some information is displayed: how large the file is (which affects download time), the date the file was first posted, which operating system it works on, and other requirements, including the price, if any. You pay for games on an honor system. If you don't pay, you receive reminder messages. When you do pay, you're given a registration number, and the program no longer reminds you to pay.

   If you're not lucky, you see the dreadfully disappointing `Sorry, no matches were found` message. Try searching for another game. This time, use a more generic term in your search (for example, **card games**).

6. Click the download button to download the file. After clicking the Download button, you might instantly be faced with the Downloading dialog box. You might see another Web page offering more information and perhaps a choice of download links.

7. Follow the Web page's information; then click a download site. The File Download dialog box appears.

8. Choose Save this program to disk. You do not want to run the program; you want to save it to your hard drive.

9. Click OK.

10. Choose a folder on your hard drive to save the file into. You can, at this point, make a special "Downloads" folder to put this new file. It makes finding the new file easier.

11. Click OK after choosing the proper disk drive and folder. A dialog box appears while you wait for the file to download. This could take some time, or it could be pretty quick depending on your modem's speed and the file's size. You see the Download Complete dialog box when the downloading is finished.

12. Click Close to close the dialog box. You're finished with the first part.

Be sure that you don't disconnect from the Internet while you're downloading a game (or anything else for that matter). Disconnecting from the Internet interrupts the download.

The file is now saved to disk, most likely in your Download folder or whatever folder you chose from the Save As dialog box when you downloaded the file. *See also* Part V for more information about creating and organizing folders.

Unarchiving a downloaded file

The file you downloaded is probably an *archive*, or a collection of many files, stuffed into a single, smaller file for quick downloading. Your next task is to unarchive the file and install the software.

Follow these steps to unarchive a file and run its Setup program:

1. Locate the downloaded file's icon. This is when you have to remember where you placed the file when you were downloading it.

2. Double-click the icon to open the file. If you're lucky, the downloaded file is a program that automatically unarchives itself and runs a Setup program. Otherwise, the downloaded file is probably a Zip file, and you need an Unzip program to extract the file from the archive.

3. After opening the file, the Setup program should run. If not, locate the Setup icon and run it to install the program.

From this point, you're on your own. Each program has its own installation procedure, which is easy enough to follow if you've been using a computer for awhile. Try to install the new program in its own folder in the Program Files folder so that you don't lose it amongst all the folders in Windows.

Zip files are called *archives,* which is one file that holds several other files as a compact unit, giving it the ability to hold a lot of information. After you download a Zip file, you need to "unzip" it, which is basically expanding all the information out again. You need a Zip file manager, such as WinZip, to do all this compacting and expanding of files. You can go to www.winzip.com to find WinZip.

Playing Games

Windows provides you with some fun games. They aren't nearly as nifty as those you can get off the Internet, but they suffice in a moment of desperation.

Follow these steps to find the games stored on your computer:

1. Click the Start button.

2. Choose Programs.

3. Choose Accessories.

4. Choose Games. The Games submenu appears, and you see a list of the games installed with Windows.

5. Click the game you want to start. May I suggest that you try Solitaire first because most people already know how to play it. However, FreeCell is my favorite and can be pretty addictive.

See also Part VIII for information on adding games to your computer.

Be aware that some corporations are banning games from employee computers. These games have taken away from valuable work time to the point that it's become a real problem. So think twice before installing games on your work computer.

Hearts

Hearts on the computer is the same traditional game you grew up with, and you play by the same traditional rules. It's also a great network game that you can play on the Internet or on a network.

Here are some Hearts hints:

- Click a card to pass or play.

- You pass three cards at the beginning of most hands. Once you pass the cards to the left, once to the right, once across, and then you keep all your cards.

- The two of clubs always leads the first hand.

- The computer always knows when you try to run them, so don't do it unless you really can and no one stops you. If you don't know what the term "try to run them" means, get with a friend and learn the game first or the computer will absolutely beat you.

- The object of the game: Don't get any hearts!

Solitaire

Think twice before learning how to play Solitaire. It is addictive!

Here are some Solitaire hints to improve your game:

- You click face-down cards to turn them over.

- Drag cards from one column to another, putting red cards on black cards in descending order.

- Double-click cards to put them on the appropriate suit pile — as in the stack of hearts, clubs, spades, or diamonds.

- You can drag whole columns or just parts of columns.

- Choose Game from the menu bar and then choose the Options command to add variety to your game.

Minesweeper

I don't understand or like Minesweeper. Let me clarify. I don't understand the fun in this game. I know, I'm probably the only one in the world who doesn't enjoy the process of trying to tiptoe through a minefield.

Here is the premise of the game: Minesweeper is composed of a grid over several hidden mines. You can click any tile in the grid to try to find a mine. If you find a mine — Boom! — you blow up. If you don't find a mine, you may see a number that tells you how many tiles in the grid around that spot have mines under them. And on top of all this, you're being timed. Okay, is this fun yet?

Follow these steps to play Minesweeper:

1. To start a new game, click Bob (the smiley face).

2. Click blank tiles.

3. When you think you've found a mine, right-click that tile. This marks the tile with a little flag.

4. If you find a mine, all the hidden mines are shown and Bob dies. Then he's not a smiley face anymore. Game over.

5. When you've found all the mines, the clock stops and Bob sports sunglasses. Game over.

You can set the size of the minefield by choosing various options in the Game menu:

✔ Beginner

✔ Intermediate

✔ Expert

✔ Custom

Each size is larger with more mines to uncover. If you win, you get to enter your name into the high score sheet. Yeehaw!

FreeCell

FreeCell is a distant cousin to Solitaire. Unlike Solitaire, where you can be defeated by a bad shuffle, every single FreeCell game has a solution, sometimes several solutions.

In FreeCell, you don't drag cards with the mouse. Instead, you click a card to select it, and then click where you want the card to move. The cards are moved with the same rules as Solitaire (higher to lower, black on red, red on black). The game tells you whether it's a valid move or not. If you can move a stack of cards to an empty slot, the game asks if you want to move the whole stack or just the top card.

Here are some FreeCell hints:

✔ Try to find the aces and move them up first.

✔ Look for trouble spots, such as three of a kind in a row. This is usually a bad sign, unless you can play all three cards.

✔ Try not to fill up the free cells with high cards (jacks, queens, and kings).

✔ If you can clear one whole column, you're halfway to winning the game.

✔ Try to look several moves in advance.

Playing with Music

New computers typically come with a great sound system. I often pop a CD into the computer and listen to music while I work.

Follow these steps to play a CD on your computer:

1. Insert the CD in your CD-ROM. Often, this brings up the CD player, and the music starts automatically. If it doesn't, you have to start the CD player manually.

2. Click the Start button.

3. Choose Programs.

4. Choose Accessories.

5. Choose Entertainment.

6. Choose CD Player.

7. Click the Play button. This is the same type of button you find on any CD player.

8. And then you have music!

Playing with Sound

The invention of the sound card brought a whole new element of fun to computers. Now game players can hear the crunch of army boots and the "Ho, ho, ho," of Santa in Elf Bowling.

Nearly every PC today has a nice sound system. If you're not sure whether your computer has a sound system — or a sound card that makes the sound system work — you can check for yourself.

Your PC should have sound connectors on its rump if it has a sound card installed. You should be able to find three tiny jacks — called *mini-din* — that accept a tiny ⅛-inch audio plug. The jacks are labeled Mic, Line in, Line out, or Speakers.

If your PC has the jacks, it can produce sound.

Speakers

Your computer needs speakers so that you can hear the sounds the sound card makes. Most PCs come with speakers or offer them as an option. If you didn't get speakers as an option, you can buy a set between $10 and $80 at your local computer store.

Here are my speaker recommendations:

✔ External speakers are better than the built-into-the-monitor type.

✔ Run your speakers electrically instead of through batteries.

✔ Subwoofers aren't necessary, but they give the bass sound a nice quality.

Speakers contain magnets. This means that you must keep floppy disks away from them, or the floppies may lose their data.

Windows sounds

Windows has a sound scheme just like it has a desktop theme. You can change all the dings and bings that Windows currently makes to something really goofy.

Follow these steps to change the Windows sounds:

1. Click the Start button.

2. Choose Settings.

3. Choose Control Panel.

4. Double-click the Sounds icon to open the Sounds Properties dialog box.

5. Click an entry in the Events drop-down list to specify which task you want to assign a particular sound to. This box lists the various tasks that Windows and some of your applications do, and you can apply a specific sound to each of these things. For example, when you exit Windows, you can have the sound of the wind blowing or the sound of someone walking.

6. Choose a sound from the Name drop-down list in the Sound area.

7. Pluck out a sound scheme in the Schemes area if you want to apply a particular scheme to the sounds for all your tasks. A *scheme* is a collection of sounds that came with Windows or the Plus! package.

8. Click OK when you have selected all the sounds that you want to use.

Recording your voice

You can record your voice on your PC if you have a microphone and the correct software. Recording software may come with your PC or sound card, or you can use a Windows program called Sound Recorder.

Follow these steps to record your voice:

1. Click the Start button.

2. Choose Programs.

3. Choose Accessories.

4. Choose Entertainment.

5. Choose Sound Recorder.

6. Get ready at the microphone, and then click the Record button.

7. Start talking, singing, or whatever.

8. Click the Stop button when you're finished.

9. Click the Play button to hear yourself.

You save the sounds you record, like you save any file. *See also* Part III for more information about saving a file.

Setting the Date and Time

Most computers come with an internal, battery-operated clock. The battery enables your computer to keep track of the time, even when your computer is off.

The current time is located at the far-right side of the Windows taskbar. If you point the mouse at the time, Windows displays the current date.

Follow these steps if you don't see the time:

1. Click the Start button.

2. Choose Settings.

3. Choose Taskbar & Start Menu.

4. Click the Taskbar Options tab to bring that panel forward.

5. Click the Show Clock option to place a check mark in the box.

6. Click OK. You should now see the time in the far-right corner of the taskbar.

Computers don't really do a good job of keeping accurate time. No one knows why, but they don't. So, you may need to set or change the date on your computer periodically.

Follow these steps to change the time or date:

1. Double-click the time on the right end of the taskbar. This displays the Date/Time Properties dialog box, as shown in the following figure. (You can also right-click the time on the taskbar, and then choose Adjust Date/Time.)

2. Highlight the time displayed, and type the new time.

3. Click the Apply button in the Date/Time Properties dialog box to set the time instantly.

4. Click OK when you're finished.

Using Two Monitors

Your PC can handle two or more monitors with Windows 98, but you have to have the proper hardware installed.

You adjust the two monitors for color and resolution in the Display Properties dialog box. Right-click the desktop, choose Properties from the shortcut menu, and the Display Properties dialog box appears. Click the Settings tab to bring that panel forward, and the window shows that you have two monitors connected.

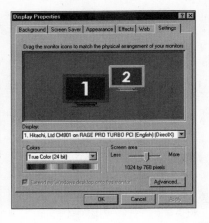

You can drag the monitor's images inside the dialog box to position them left, right, or on top of each other. The numbers on each monitor correspond to the monitors listed in the drop-down Display list.

The point of all this is to give you more screen area. For example, as I write, I keep my outline on one monitor and my chapters on the other monitor.

Here are some hints to help you get the most from using more than one monitor:

✔ Find the file in the Windows folder on drive C called display.txt. Open that file and read the information about which video adapters are supported for dual monitors.

✔ If the second monitor is recognized, Windows displays a text message on it when your PC starts.

✔ To activate a monitor, click its icon in the Display Properties dialog box. Click Yes if you're asked to enable the monitor.

✔ The desktop image appears on both monitors.

✔ Windows can be dragged from one monitor to the other. Just click and drag.

✔ Games will run only on your main monitor.

✔ You have to minimize a window before you can drag it across to the monitor.

Follow these steps to add a second monitor:

1. Remove your PC's first adapter.

2. Add the second adapter.

3. Configure the second adapter.

4. Re-install the first adapter.

By installing one monitor at a time this way, you avoid the biggest problem that often comes with installing a second monitor: the ability of Windows to find the proper driver (software). For some reason, Windows finds the drivers best working one at a time.

Working with Fonts

A font is a type style. It defines the way text looks both on-screen and when your document is printed. Windows comes with a host of fonts, and you can add your own to the mix. By using fonts carefully and creatively, you can add weight or spice to any document you create, even if it's something like a chore chart for your kids.

Finding fonts

Fonts are basically collected in one location. Working with and organizing fonts is fairly easy because they are all held in one place.

Follow these steps to find the fonts:

1. Click the Start button.

2. Choose Settings.

3. Choose Control Panel.

4. Double-click the Fonts folder. What you see doesn't really tell you much, except that each name is a type of font.

5. Click the X to close the folder.

Using fonts

Fonts are applied to any text you write in Windows. Typically, the Font command is found in the Format menu, although some programs use a toolbar drop-down list of fonts. If you change a font, that change applies to any selected text; if no text is selected, the change applies to any new text you type.

The font's name describes the font's overall appearance.

```
The Courier font is a basic, easy-to-read typing font.
```

The Courier font is an example of a *monospaced* font. Each character takes up the same space as other characters in the font. So, a capital *M* is as wide as the lowercase *i*.

The Times font is popular for text and easy to read.

Times is an example of a proportionally spaced font, which is easy to read and professional-looking. Each character takes up only as much space as it needs to.

Times is also an example of a *serif* font. The characters have small feet on the ends of the characters, which are called *serifs*. They make reading the characters easier.

Arial is a font normally used for headings and titles.

Arial is an example of a *sans serif* font, which lacks the tiny feet of a serif font. These fonts are best suited for headlines and titles. Because they are harder to read, sans serif fonts aren't well suited to text.

Besides the techie descriptions of a font as either serif or sans serif, fonts can also have *attributes*. Attributes include **bold,** *italics,* a ***combination of both,*** or underline.

Font size

Fonts have size. That size is measured in points, and there are 72 points to an inch. The typical size for most regular body text is either 10 or 12 points, which is a good reading size.

Font names

You use different types of fonts for different purposes. The following list describes some of the font types that you find in the Fonts folder:

- **TrueType font:** These fonts appear on-screen exactly as they appear when you print them. They can be stretched or shrunk to any size.

- **Open-type font:** An improvement on the basic TrueType font, it looks even better in various font sizes.

- **Type 1, vector and raster font:** This type of font is known as a *screen* font or *fixed* font, and is an older type used primarily by early Windows applications. Type 1 fonts look good only in a few sizes (typically 10, 12, and 15 points).

Other types of fonts exist as well. For example, your computer may have PostScript fonts, which are designed for use with PostScript printers. These fonts typically live in another folder and have their own utility for font management.

Previewing new fonts

Double-click the font's icon in the Fonts folder to preview the font. You see a special Quick View window displaying all sorts of details.

Click the X (Close) button when you finish looking at the fonts.

Adding fonts from a CD-ROM or floppy disk

New fonts are added to your system using a special command in the Fonts window. You can actually add fonts from one of three places:

✔ From a fonts CD-ROM or floppy disk

✔ From a network, if you're connected to one

✔ From the Internet

Follow these steps to add fonts from a CD-ROM or disk:

1. Insert the floppy disk or CD-ROM. Yes, you need to already have a CD-ROM or floppy disk of fonts. Computer supply stores have a ton of font CDs that you can buy, and they're fairly inexpensive.

2. Click the Start button.

3. Choose Settings.

4. Choose Control Panel.

5. Double-click the Fonts icon.

6. Choose File from the menu bar.

7. Choose Install New Font.

8. Find the fonts. Where are you getting these fonts? If you have a disk or CD, click the drive name. For example, fonts coming from a floppy disk would be in drive A. It takes Windows a little while to read in the font names, but then a list of fonts appears in the window.

9. Use one of the following methods to select the fonts that you want to add:

   • Press Ctrl+click to select individual fonts (hold down the Ctrl key while you click each font individually).

   • Click the Select All button if you want to select all the fonts that are offered.

10. Click OK. Windows shows you a brief dialog box that says your fonts are being loaded. You can find them listed in your Fonts window after they are loaded.

Adding fonts from a network

If your computer is on a network, it is hooked (by cable) to someone else's computer. Networks are fun because you can share the information that they contain. So if the guy down the hall has all these really cool fonts, you can get on your computer, find his fonts, and then copy them over to your computer.

Follow these steps to add new fonts from a network:

1. Open the Fonts folder. ***Remember:*** Click Start, choose Settings⇨Control Panel, and then double-click the Fonts icon.

2. Choose File from the menu bar.

3. Choose Install New Font.

4. Click the Network button. The Map Network Drive box is displayed.

5. Click the down arrow next to Drive and find the Drive and Path where the new fonts live.

6. Click OK.

7. Work through the list of folders to find the file that contains the fonts. This is easier if you know exactly where the fonts are living. You may even have to go to your buddy down the hall and say, "Hey Buddy, I want to share those new fonts you just got. Where are they hiding?"

8. Click the file where the fonts are hiding to highlight it and then click OK.

9. Select the fonts that you want to keep. Remember that to select individual font files, you can hold down the Ctrl key while you click the fonts you want.

10. Click OK. Windows shows you a brief dialog box that says your fonts are being loaded. You can find them listed in your Fonts window after they are loaded.

Printing fonts

If you like to try different styles of fonts, you may want to print a hard copy of all your fonts. This saves you the repeated process of opening and closing each font to see what it looks like.

Follow these steps to print fonts:

1. Open the Fonts folder. ***Remember:*** Click Start, choose Settings⇨Control Panel, and then double-click the Fonts icon.

2. Double-click a font to open the preview window.

3. Click the Print button to choose a printer.

4. Choose your printer.

5. Click OK.

You have to go through each font and work through this process with each one. After they're all printed, put them in a file folder or binder for easy access.

Removing fonts

You may find that some fonts are just too ugly or boring to use in any of your documents. Fine. Just get rid of the darn thing. But be respectful of fonts you are borrowing from the network. Don't delete a font from someone else's file. That's just not right.

Follow these steps to delete a font:

1. Open the Fonts folder. *Remember:* Click Start, choose Settings⇨Control Panel, and then double-click the Fonts icon.

2. Select the font or fonts that you want to delete by clicking on each one.

3. Choose File from the menu bar.

4. Choose Delete. Alternately, you can press the delete key. A warning box appears, asking if you're sure that you want to delete the font.

5. Click Yes. The font is deleted.

PC Tips and Golden Rules

The best and happiest computer users are the ones who live and breathe by the tips in this part. These are suggestions that have been touched on throughout this book, and they are key to a happy relationship with your computer. The last thing anyone wants is for you to lug your computer over to the window and toss the darned thing out because of your frustration with it. So give yourself a break and keep these PC Golden Rules in mind.

In this part . . .

Back Up Your Files

If you rely on your computer for your livelihood, or if your PC contains files that would be difficult, time-consuming, or impossible to recreate, you owe it to yourself to perform regular back ups. Computers *will* mess up. They'll freeze and crash and do all those horrible things you hear about, all when you least expect it or when it's particularly inconvenient. It's true that some folks never experience these problems; the more you work on your computer, however, the more likely it is that someday, somewhere, when you least expect it, you will experience some type of data loss. Develop a solid back-up routine now so that you're prepared for that dreaded day. *See also* Part X to find out more about backing up your data.

Buy a UPS

An uninterruptible power supply (UPS) keeps all those little power surges and bleeps from affecting the performance of your computer. Some places (where we live, for example) constantly have little power burps. We know this because our UPS devices always give out little beeps when the power fluctuates. At a certain point in time, these power burps will shut down your computer, causing you to lose any unsaved information. Worse still is the extreme frustration of having your computer randomly shut off while you're working.

A UPS can be purchased anywhere computers are sold.

One additional little thing that you can do to avoid heartache and frustration when the power fluctuates is to save your work frequently! Most applications have a key combination that you can press quickly to save your work. In Microsoft Word, for example, all you have to do is press Ctrl+S to save your work to your hard drive. If you can get in the habit of pressing that key combination every few minutes or every couple of paragraphs (if you're writing text), it can save you a great deal of time if your computer shuts down suddenly from a power surge. And don't forget the quick motion of reaching that mouse up and clicking on the save button on the toolbar.

Buy Enough Supplies

You will run out of everything: paper, printer cartridges, floppy disks, and so on, usually at the most inconvenient time. Buy a supply now, so you don't have to stop what you're doing to run to the store to pick this stuff up.

Clean Your Computer

Maintaining your computer goes a long way in keeping it running smoothly. Don't be shy or lazy about doing the maintenance tasks recommended in Part IX. Your computer will be more efficient if you keep your drives happy by performing routine maintenance.

Continue to Educate Yourself

The more you know about computers and the software available, the more you can do. You can create some very impressive documents, play more advanced games, and even create art! The possibilities are amazing, but you have to continue to learn.

We're here to help, too. If you want to find other books written by Dan Gookin and Sandra Hardin Gookin, check out our title list at www.wambooli.com/. Click the Publications — Books link.

Don't Buy Too Much Software

Is it possible to have too much software? That may seem like asking whether it's possible to have too much money.

Your computer probably came with some software programs already installed for you. Before you go on a shopping spree, find out what you have and play around with those programs to see if they meet your needs. Software takes a while to learn, so give yourself some time to get acquainted with what you have before you lay down your credit card at the local computer store.

Ensure That Your Hardware Is Compatible

Do your research and read those boxes before you buy! Not all hardware works with all computers. Maybe you thought you were getting a great deal on a USB modem, only to find that your computer doesn't have a USB port. Or perhaps you bought an AGP expansion card, but all you have are PCI slots. These terms may sound like gibberish to you right now, but if you take a careful inventory of your current system (now's the time to pull out those manuals that came with your PC) and carefully research what components are compatible, this terminology will begin to make sense and you won't end up with cool, new gadgets that won't work with your system.

Get Comfortable

Put everything in place so that working at your computer is a comfortable experience. Follow these comfort tips:

- Adjust the monitor to fit your comfort level. Monitors that are too dark or too light cause eye strain.

- Buy an ergonomic chair. Comfort and proper positioning are the keys to avoiding back and neck problems. If you're not sure about the correct sitting position, go to an office supply store and have yourself fitted for a chair.

- Buy a computer desk. The keyboard needs to be at a proper level so that your shoulders and wrists don't start hurting from improper positioning.

- Read the Appendix, "Ten Things Worth Buying for Your PC" for more ideas about items that can increase your comfort level.

Leave SPAM E-Mail Alone

SPAM e-mail generates more SPAM e-mail if you respond to it. That means that even if you respond to the e-mail asking to be taken off their mailing list (which they always tell you to do if you don't want to receive their messages), this simply confirms that you are there — which means you'll get more SPAM e-mail.

Leave Strange Disks Alone

Using someone else's disk to load software or to start your computer is the best way to get a computer virus. Unless you bought the software or you personally made the disk (and it's always been in your possession), leave the disk alone.

Leave Unknown Things Alone

This bit of advice pertains to both hardware and software. Live by these rules:

- If you didn't create that file you just found on your computer, don't delete it.

- Don't physically open anything (boxes, cases, and so on) attached to your PC unless you know what you're doing.

Quit Windows Properly

You can leave your computer on pretty much all the time. No law or rule says that you have to turn your computer off every time you stop working. But if you do want to turn your computer off, shut it down properly.

Don't just flip off the power switch when you're finished working. (Read the shut down process in "The Big Picture" section.) Don't use the reset button unless everything is frozen and you can't do anything else. Flipping the switch and using the reset button are used too much, and your hard drive doesn't like it. **See also** "The Basics: Turning Off the Computer" in "The Big Picture" section for more information about safely shutting down your PC.

Save Your Work

Save. Save. Save. Get in the habit of reaching your mouse up and clicking that Save button every few minutes, or find out your application's keyboard shortcut for saving. In Microsoft Word, for example, you can press Ctrl+S to quickly save your work to your hard drive. Living in a paranoid state is awful, but at least it's safe.

Subscribe to a Computer Magazine

Family PC is a good magazine for products that relate to family issues, such as software reviews and educational software topics. If you want to get into the really technical topics, *PC World* can probably quench your thirst for techno-news. Reading computer magazines helps you stay up-to-date on the latest technology and computer trends. If you're informed, you won't be intimidated into upgrading or trading your computer based on rumors that you hear. Information is power!

access: The ability to get into something or to locate something. You may gain access to disks, records, files, and networks.

active area: A region of the screen or window that is accepting input from the user.

address book: A place to store your electronic mail names and addresses. "My *address book* is filled with all the most popular geeks, thanks to online dating."

Alt key: A special type of key on computer keyboards, often used in combination with other keys to give commands to the computer. Common commands are Alt+F to access the File menu and Alt+E to access the Edit menu.

application programs: The programs on a computer that do the work. Application programs include word processors, spreadsheets, and databases.

arrow keys: Special keys on the keyboard that move the cursor up, down, left, or right. Not surprisingly, the arrow keys have little arrows on them. These keys are also referred to as *cursor keys.* "Bill just quit tech support. He told a lady to press the up-arrow key, and she shot back at him that there were 12 arrows on her keyboard, 5 of which pointed up."

asterisk: The * symbol on the keyboard.

background: A multitasking term that indicates a program is running a "task" that you're not currently working with or have visible on the screen. Most printing takes place in the background.

backspace: 1. The key on the keyboard that has the word Backspace on it. This key might also have a left-pointing arrow on it. 2. The act of pressing the Backspace key, which deletes something. In a word processor, the Backspace key erases the character immediately to the left of the cursor.

backup set: A collection of files and folders (and any other data) that have been backed up and stored on a file or tape.

bold: In word processing or desktop publishing, the attribute applied to text that **darkens** it.

boot: 1. To start a computer. 2. To load a specific operating system.

boot disk: The disk you use to start your computer. Most often, this refers to a hard drive, although a floppy disk with the proper operating system installed can also boot a computer.

bug: A problem that prevents a program from working properly. Typically unexpected, a bug is something that nearly every program has.

bundled software: 1. Software that comes free (supposedly) when you buy a computer. Usually, bundled software is stuff you need or programs that aren't selling well, so the publisher is trying to give it away just to clean out a warehouse. Most computers offer bundled software, such as Microsoft Office. The idea is that you pay half as much money for twice as much software, two-thirds of which you don't need anyway. 2. Several different programs that come together as one package, such as Microsoft Works.

cable: A connector, typically one that has electronic signals flowing through it, hither and thither. Cables connect different parts so that they actually do something useful. Cables can be either internal or external to the computer box.

CD-ROM: Acronym for Compact Disc-Read Only Memory. CD-ROMs are discs that contain megabytes of information.

central processing unit: The computer's microprocessor, abbreviated CPU. The CPU is the little chip in a personal computer that controls everything. It's about the size of a thin wafer or a headless cockroach.

character: Any symbol that you can type from the keyboard. Letters are characters, numbers are characters, and even $, @, _, ^, and ~ are considered characters.

Clipboard: A temporary storage area for items that have been cut or copied. Use the Paste command to place a copy of the item from the Clipboard into the current application. The Clipboard can hold text, graphics, or other objects.

close: To remove a window from the screen in a graphical operating system. To finish working on a document, remove it from the screen, and optionally save it to disk. Close can also mean to quit a program.

console: The main computer box; the thing that all the other parts of your computer plug into.

Control key: A special key, abbreviated Ctrl on most keyboards. The Control key works with other keys to give commands to a program. For example, Ctrl+S in many programs is the keyboard shortcut for saving a file.

Control Panel: The place to go to customize your desktop and other aspects of your computer.

data: Information people think is important and useful to save.

delete: To remove a file from a disk; to erase or kill the file.

desktop: What appears on your monitor after you have Windows up and running. Icons are placed on the desktop for easy access to their programs.

Dial-up networking: Provides a connection between your computer and the Internet, a network, or another computer.

display: The monitor or computer screen, specifically the information shown there.

driver file: A driver is a type of program, which is a file on disk. The driver (program) is designed to control a specific piece of hardware, interfacing between the hardware and the operating system and, eventually, the user. For example, you need a driver to operate the printer. Each printer has its own driver file that controls the printer, talks to the operating system, and handles all the printer's details.

double-click: To press the left (or primary) mouse button twice in rapid succession without moving the mouse between clicks.

DNS: Acronym for Domain Name Service, software that runs on an Internet computer that converts Internet names and addresses into actual locations on the Internet. The DNS Server is a computer (or a program running on that computer) that translates weird Internet stuff you type into the real (and cryptic) addresses.

drag: To move an on-screen object with the mouse. First, you highlight (select) the object that you want by pointing to it with the mouse. Then you hold down the mouse button and move the mouse. This drags the object around.

driver: A program that gives a device (such as a printer or a disk drive) direction on how to work. The driver, as well as the peripheral, must be activated within the extension folder.

DVD: Acronym for Digital Versatile Disk (sometimes called Digital Video Disk). A high-speed CD-ROM that holds up to 17MB of information — enough for a feature-length movie — as opposed to the 600MB of a traditional CD. Some computers use DVD-RAM drives for backup.

e-mail: Short for electronic mail.

eject: To remove a disk from a disk drive.

Enter key: A key on the keyboard named Enter. This key is often used to signal the computer that you're finished typing a command; only after pressing the Enter key is your text sent to the computer.

erase: To remove a file from a disk.

error message: A cryptic note that the computer displays to let you know that the program isn't working right, or that you've really screwed up.

fax: Short for facsimile copy machine; a device that sends a printed page through the phone lines to another machine that prints a copy.

file: The basic chunk of information stored on a computer disk. Files can be programs, text, raw data, or graphics.

folder: Another name for a subdirectory.

font: A collection of characters with predefined sizes and style. Most word processors and desktop publishing programs let you choose different fonts to make your writing prettier.

function keys: A set of keys that serve a variety of purposes, depending on the program. These are the keys named F1 through F10 (or F12), and are generally located along the top of your keyboard.

game: The only type of program that people really buy a computer for. Game programs fall into three categories: arcade, strategy, and board.

glitch: A problem (sometimes temporary) that causes a program to work erratically or not at all. Glitches can also be called *bugs*.

graphics: Artwork; anything non-text on a computer.

hard copy: Printed information.

hardware: The physical part of a computer; anything you can touch and see.

Help system: The Windows system that is used to display information (helpful information) about Windows.

Home page: The Web site that your computer automatically goes to each time you connect to the Internet. You may also return to this site automatically by clicking the Home button, located at the top of your screen.

icon: A symbol that looks like Egyptian hieroglyphics, often used in place of actual words. Many programs display icons as shortcuts to choosing commands through menus. Instead of choosing a menu command, you can just click the mouse on the icon, as long as you remember which icon represents which command.

inkjet printer: A type of printer that sprays ink on paper, instead of smacking an inked ribbon against the page, like an impact printer does. Inkjet printers are quieter than dot-matrix printers, producing better quality printing as well (but not as good as laser printers).

Internet: A collection of computers all over the world that send, receive, and store information. The Internet is not a single computer. It is not a software program. It's merely a lot of computers communicating with each other.

ISP: Acronym for Internet Service Provider. A commercial organization that provides dial-up access to the Internet, like a cable company for computer users who want to get on the Internet. Often called ISPs, an Internet service provider is already connected to the Internet. An ISP provides you with an access code and phone number, which you use to get on the Internet.

italic: In word processing or desktop publishing, the attribute applied to text that *slants* it.

key: The buttons on the keyboard.

keyboard: The device that you use to communicate with the computer. You mostly interact with the computer by typing on the keyboard.

keyboard shortcut: A single key or combination of keys that activates a command. Specifically, this refers to the shortcut shown in a menu, such as Ctrl+V; Ctrl+V is the keyboard shortcut for pasting something from the Clipboard into a document.

laptop: A computer that is small enough to fit in your lap without crushing your kneecaps in the process.

laser printer: A type of printer that uses a laser beam to generate an image and electronically transfer it to paper. The speed of a laser printer is measured in how many pages per minute (ppm) it can produce.

memory: Information storage inside a computer.

menu: A list of commands or options available within a program. Menus show you options in a list.

microprocessor: The central processing chip in a microcomputer. Common microprocessors include the Motorola 68000, 68030, 68040 used in Macintoshes, and the Intel 286, 386, 486, and Pentium chips used in PCs. The microprocessor controls most of the core functions of the computer but can be enhanced with coprocessor chips.

modem: The device that enables your computer to connect to the Internet, as well as to send and receive information from other computers over the phone line.

monitor: Another name for a CRT, screen, or terminal. It's that thing you stare into for hours on end when using your computer.

motherboard: The main circuit board of a computer, to which most devices connect. The motherboard is the real estate upon which the computer's CPU, ROM chips, and often the RAM chips sit and work. It also contains the expansion slots and other electronic doodads, making it look like an electronic sushi display.

mouse: A pointing device used to provide input for the computer. Most graphical user interfaces (Windows and the Macintosh) use mouse input devices. When you move the mouse on your desk, the mouse pointer on the screen mimics its movement. This allows you to control, point at, grab, and manipulate various graphics goodies (and text) in a program.

My Computer: An icon representing the contents of your PC — all the disk drives, printers, plus other folders — in Windows.

newsgroups: A discussion area (group) on USENET. A forum where people can read or write their own news, messages, and flames. Newsgroups have a certain hierarchical format, which replaces spaces with periods. The first word describes a general category, such as a "comp" for computers or "talk" for general discussions. Then comes a subcategory and maybe even more categories.

network: A system of computers connected to each other for data transfer, communications, and sharing of application programs.

numeric keypad: The portion of the keyboard that contains the number keys, usually all grouped into rows and columns by themselves.

online: Another way of saying that you are connected to the Internet. You must be online to do anything on the Internet, such as shopping, checking e-mail, or researching information.

open: To access a program or file, just as you would open a book if you wanted to read it.

operating system: The software that controls the hardware and also runs your programs.

Page Down key: A glorified cursor key that moves you forward (down) in the document the exact length of your screen every time you press it.

Page Up key: A key on the keyboard that moves the cursor up (backward) through your document to the top, one screen length page at a time.

paste: The tool used for taking information from other sources (that were either copied or cut) and putting that information into another document or into another place in the same document.

pathname: The full name of a file. The pathname includes the drive where the file lives, the folders in which the file is saved, and then the file itself. The drive letter is followed by a colon and backslash that separate the folder names. For example, C:\My Documents\Theatre\Productions\ new season.

PC: Acronym for personal computer.

pointer: A symbol that appears on the screen and corresponds to the movement of the mouse or other pointing device. The pointer doesn't always look the same. It can take on different guises in different applications or even in different functions within the same application.

portable computer: A PC you can carry around with you without making yourself a candidate for the trauma ward. These include laptops, notebooks, and hand-held computers.

portal site: A main site on the Internet with lots to offer; generally tries to position itself as a *home page,* or starting point for visitors to the Web. Usually contains a search engine, shopping, games, news, sports, weather, e-mail, and other information that makes you want to visit. Some examples of portal sites include yahoo.com and excite.com.

power strips: A device containing several power sockets, designed like an extension cord and used to plug in the myriad of devices surrounding your computer.

printer: An output device for the computer. A printer allows you to obtain a hard copy of the stuff you create inside the computer. This is the end result of your PC labors.

RAM: Acronym for Random-Access Memory, a type of computer memory that can be written to and read from. The "random" means that any one location can be read at any time; it's not necessary to read all the memory to find one location. RAM commonly refers to the internal memory of your computer, supplied by microchips and measured in kilobytes or megabytes. However, RAM can refer to any random-access memory medium, including magnetic disks and the human brain. RAM is usually a fast, temporary memory area where your data and programs live until you save them or the power to your computer is turned off.

redo: To repeat the last action that you undid. For example, if you accidentally delete text with the Undo command, you can use redo to bring back the deleted text (instead of retyping it).

resolution: A way of measuring the clarity of an image.

save: To store data in a permanent form, typically on a disk drive.

scan: To read text, images, or bar codes into the computer.

screen saver: A special program that periodically blanks out the screen and replaces it with utter darkness or often some form of graphic or entertainment. Screen savers prevent the same image from appearing on your screen and being "burned-in" permanently.

scroll bar: The gizmo used to scroll up or down, or right or left, through a document, Web page, or e-mail letter. The *vertical* scroll bar, located at the right of the screen, lets you scroll up or down. The *horizontal* scroll bar, located at the bottom of the screen, lets you scroll side to side.

search engine: A program that searches the Internet for topics or key words. The search engine will list this information, like an encyclopedia.

Shift key: A modifier key primarily used to produce uppercase letters on the keyboard.

software: The brains of the computer. Software tells the hardware what to do.

submenu: A menu that appears after you choose an item from the primary menu.

tape drive: A machine into which you insert a tape cassette that records data. The machine is like a tape recorder, reading and writing information to the tape. Many folks use the tape drive to backup data. There's usually no swapping involved, and the backup takes only a few minutes. A tape drive is about as expensive as a new hard drive, and several formats are available, including ¼-inch cartridge, 8-mm VCR cartridge, 4-mm audio, and 9-track.

taskbar: A strip of buttons along the bottom of the Windows desktop. Each button relates to a window or an on-screen task, allowing you to switch between the tasks by clicking the button. The Start button and the system tray are also on the taskbar.

text: Stuff that you've typed into a document. Letters, numbers, and other characters or symbols found on your keyboard create text.

tower PC: A desktop computer on its side, but really a computer that was made to stand vertically (up and down). These computers usually have more room and tend to be more powerful than mere mortal desktop models.

undelete: To put something back the way it was before you deleted it.

underline: In word processing or desktop publishing, the attribute applied to text that makes it look like it has a line under it.

undo: To retract the last action you did, whether that was adding or deleting text or applying bold or italics.

utility: Software intended to help you fix, tweak, or enhance your system.

version: An edition of a product. Versions are usually designated with a number, such as "Crash-o-Matic 2.0 for Windows," in which 2.0 indicates that it is the second edition of the original release.

virus: A nasty type of program created by nasty people. A virus is capable of replicating itself and doing severe damage to the contents of other users' systems.

Web browser: Software designed to view documents written in HTML, which includes all pages on the World Wide Web. There are two popular Web browers, one from Netscape and the other from Microsoft. Web browsers display information on the Internet using text, graphics, sounds and all sorts of interesting distractions. They can also display Gopher, FTP, and newsgroup information.

window: An area on the screen that displays data, programs, or information. A window can be moved, resized, opened, and closed, allowing you to organize the data on your computer screen.

zoom: To enlarge or reduce an image, typically a document displayed in a window.

Ten Things Worth Buying for Your PC

I'm not trying to sell you anything. Really. But you may want to consider buying some little things for your computer. These ten things will make working with the beast, I mean, your computer, more enjoyable.

Antiglare Screen

An antiglare screen is nothing more than a nylon stocking stretched over the front of your monitor. Okay, these are professional nylons in fancy holders that adhere themselves to your screen. The net result is no garish glare from the lights in the room or from an out-side window. It's such a good idea that some monitors come with built-in antiglare screens.

Glare is the number-one cause of eyestrain for folks using a computer.

Ergonomic Keyboard

The traditional computer keyboard is based on the old typewriter keyboard (the IBM Selectric, by the way). To help you type more comfortably, you can get an ergonomic keyboard, such as the Microsoft Natural Keyboard. These keyboards arrange the keys in a manner that's comfortable for your hands, keeping everything lined up and not tweaked out like on a regular computer keyboard. It takes some getting used to, but can be a lifesaver for tired and sore wrists.

If you have an ergonomic keyboard, you probably don't need a wrist pad. The ergonomic keyboard is shaped in such a way that typing on it isn't stressful to your wrists.

Keyboard Cover

The keyboard cover is a great idea if you're klutzy with a coffee cup or have small children with sticky fingers. (Do children ever come with clean hands?) A keyboard cover fits snugly over the keyboard but still enables you to type.

Larger or Second Monitor

Ever see a 19-inch computer monitor? How about the 21-inch model? They're wonderful. The 17-inch monitor you probably have was a good choice when you bought your computer. But check out the screen real estate on that larger monitor.

The nifty thing about Windows 98 and buying a new monitor is that you don't have to toss out the old one. You can use both monitors at once. You need a second video adapter to drive the second monitor, but it's absolutely wonderful. *See also* Part XIII to find out how to connect a second monitor.

Larger, Faster Hard Drive

Hard drives fill up quickly. The answer is to buy a larger hard drive. If you can, install a second hard drive and start filling it up. Otherwise, replace your first hard drive with a larger, faster model. Actually, buying a faster model is a great way to improve the performance of any older PC without throwing it out entirely.

More Memory

Any PC works better with more memory installed. An upper limit is anywhere from 128 to 512MB or so, which is ridiculous — well, presently. Still, upgrading your system to 32, 64, or 128MB of RAM is a good idea. Almost immediately, you notice an improvement in how Windows runs, as well as increased speed when you use graphics programs and games.

Mouse Pad and Wrist Pad

The best surface for your mouse is a mouse pad, which is a screen-sized piece of foam rubber with a textured top; ideal for rolling mice around. Avoid the mouse pads with a smooth finish.

You pay more for pads with cute pictures or the new mood pads that react to temperature.

A wrist pad fits right below your keyboard. It enables you to comfortably rest your wrists while you type and helps you avoid those nasty repetitive stress injuries that have plagued many keyboard users.

Some mouse pads even have wrist pads built in. (Yup, you're supposed to hold up your wrist when you move the mouse, too.)

Scanner or Digital Camera

If you want the latest PC toy, buy a scanner or digital camera. Scanners are wonderful if you enjoy graphics and want to send pictures over the Internet. Digital cameras are great toys, too, but they can be expensive. And you may need some time to get used to using one.

Software

Never neglect software. Jillions of different types of software programs are available, each of them designed to perform a specific task for a certain type of user. If you ever find yourself frustrated by the way the computer does something, consider looking for a piece of software that does it better.

USB Expansion Card

USB is the *thing* to have for expanding your PC. If your computer lacks a USB port, you can buy a USB expansion card. My advice: Get a two-port USB PCI card.

USB stands for Universal Serial Bus. A USB is a piece of hardware that is used to communicate between a computer and some other gadget you're connecting to your computer. The back of your computer will host a USB port, which is really the most versatile jack on the back of your computer. Windows 98 (and Windows 2000) works best with USB devices. You can use Windows 95, but you need to get special software, which usually comes with the USB card.

PCI stands for Peripheral Component Interconnect. A PCI is a piece of hardware that is used for connecting peripherals (gadgets of sorts) to a personal computer.

Index

Notes

Notes

Notes

Notes